THE AGNS PERMANENT COLLECTION
Selected Works

Contributors

Bernard Riordon, *Director and Curator of Folk Art, 1975-2002*

Ray Cronin, *Curator of Contemporary Art*

Judy Dietz, *Manager of Collections/Registrar*

Mora Dianne O'Neill, *Associate Curator Historical Prints and Drawings*

Alexandra McCurdy, *Associate Curator Ceramics*

Jim Logan, *former Associate Curator First Nations Art*

Joseph Sherman, *Editor*

ACKNOWLEDGEMENT

This publication of *The AGNS Permanent Collection–Selected Works* has been made possible by financial support from the Estate of Nelly Beveridge Gray (1907-2002).

Published by the Art Gallery of Nova Scotia
PO Box 2262
1723 Hollis Street
Halifax, Nova Scotia B3J 3C8
www.agns.gov.ns.ca

Publication Design: Fraser Ross, Semaphor Design Company
Photography: various
Film Separations: Maritime Digital Colour
Printed in Canada by: Halcraft Printers Inc.

National Library of Canada Cataloguing in Publication
Art Gallery of Nova Scotia
The AGNS permanent collection : selected works / contributors: Bernard Riordon... [et al.].
Includes index.

ISBN 0-888-71-776-8

1. Art Gallery of Nova Scotia. 2. Art--Nova Scotia--Halifax. I. Riordon, Bernard II. Title.
N910.H23A53 2002 708.11'6225 C2002-905534-2

CONTENTS

PREFACES 4 INTRODUCTION 6

CANADIAN HISTORICAL PAINTING 17

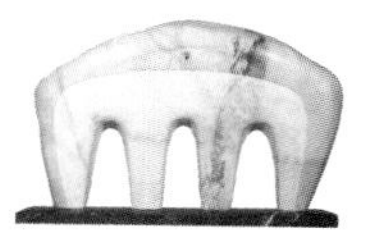

CONTEMPORARY ART 53

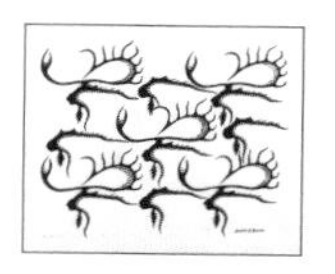

FIRST NATIONS AND INUIT ART 89

FOLK ART 105

CERAMICS 127

HISTORICAL PRINTS AND DRAWINGS 141

INTERNATIONAL PAINTING AND SCULPTURE 173

LIST OF ARTISTS 189 NOTES ON CONTRIBUTORS 190

MINISTER'S PREFACE

The Province of Nova Scotia takes great pride in the Art Gallery of Nova Scotia and supports its commitment to serving the public through the visual arts. For years, staff, volunteers, and Board members of the AGNS have provided leadership in developing and preserving collections, exhibitions, and education programs for the people of this province. The publishing of this document marks yet another significant milestone in the life story of the Gallery.

The AGNS Permanent Collection – Selected Works is more than just a published collection of the Gallery's selected permanent works of art. This book symbolizes growth, maturity, diversity, and success. In many ways, this publication paints a self-portrait of the Gallery's inspiring evolution, which was fostered and nurtured by Director and CEO Bernard Riordon, whose passion and determination have taken Nova Scotia's visual and cultural identity to new heights. *The AGNS Permanent Collection – Selected Works* is a true testament to all his efforts.

The Hon. Rodney MacDonald
Minister of Tourism and Culture
Province of Nova Scotia

CHAIR'S PREFACE

The publication of *The AGNS Permanent Collection – Selected Works* is a distinctly appropriate achievement for the Art Gallery of Nova Scotia, as a testament to the nearly thirty years in which Bernard Riordon has been Director, and as evidence of the tremendous growth of the Permanent Collection—from 200 works of art in 1973 to over 9,000 in 2002—a tribute to his leadership for which collection development has been a priority.

This huge number of works by some of the finest artists in Canada, as well as the international component, made the challenge of selecting representative works from the collection a formidable one. The staff responded with great enthusiasm, and produced an outstanding volume that puts the focus on selected works from a first-class collection, held in public trust for the people of Nova Scotia.

As with all projects of this magnitude, the seemingly endless task of accumulating and revising information was facilitated by many individuals on the Gallery's staff, and I wish to thank them for their essential participation. Thank-you to AGNS Director and CEO Bernard Riordon, also Curator of Folk Art, for his informative introduction, and for developing this wonderful collection from 1973 to the present.

Congratulations and sincere thanks to Ray Cronin, Curator of Contemporary Art; Judy Dietz, Manager of Collections/Registrar; Dr. Dianne O'Neill, Associate Curator Historical Prints and Drawings; Alexandra McCurdy, Associate Curator Ceramics; and Jim Logan, former Associate Curator First Nations Art, and the other members of the AGNS staff who assisted with this project. A special thank-you to Joseph Sherman who assisted with assembling the book in a timely way. It is a distinct privilege to acknowledge these individuals who merit our respect and gratitude.

The AGNS is deeply grateful to the many collectors, public and corporate, who have generously donated works of art over the years, during which the acquisition committees have addressed the Gallery's collecting mandate with care and due diligence. We congratulate all of the artists who are represented in this publication, and in the Art Gallery of Nova Scotia Permanent Collection. We celebrate their creative talents, and we are proud to have their works of art in trust for the people of Nova Scotia.

Don A. MacVicar, Chair
AGNS Board of Governors

INTRODUCTION

The seed that has grown into the Art Gallery of Nova Scotia of today was planted in 1908 when the province issued a charter to the Nova Scotia Museum of Fine Arts. The growth and development of the AGNS over nine decades has taken it from obscurity to a central position in the cultural, educational, and social life of Nova Scotia. The history of the Gallery has been characterized by a constant struggle to survive, a stubborn pursuit of excellence, and a long, but finally fruitful, search for a permanent home in which to display the collection of artworks that represents the cultural heritage of the people of Nova Scotia.

A Home for the Collection

Despite its lack of a physical structure to call its home, the NSMFA acquired a varied collection of over 200 works of art by local, national, and international artists, which it necessarily dispersed throughout Halifax for storage and display. The Museum's directors and its supporters never lost sight of their main objective, however, as recorded at the 1953 annual meeting:

> *"The aim of our society is constantly to be kept in the back of our minds; that someday we will be the proud owners of a museum of our own, where our collection of paintings will give joy and happiness to all the people of Nova Scotia. . . ."*

Responding to the quickening interest in local heritage generated by the country's centenary in 1967, the Province of Nova Scotia enacted legislation in 1968 to expand the scope and responsibilities of the NSMFA. The Museum took up residence at the Centennial Art Gallery, located in a 200-year-old powder magazine in the historic Halifax Citadel, and would continue to operate this gallery until January of 1978, when the facility was restored to its original function by Parks Canada. A volunteer women's committee, established that year to support the Gallery, operated a very successful Art Sales and Rental Gallery in the Cavalier Block of the Citadel, providing support for Nova Scotian artists, and much-needed revenue for the Gallery.

The increased presence of the Museum in the Halifax community, afforded by its operation of the Centennial Art Gallery, encouraged its members to consider the complete restructuring and reformation of the NSMFA as a truly provincial art gallery. In the forefront of this movement was Cdr. C. Anthony Law, whose leadership and tireless efforts brought together the volunteers and resources needed to achieve this end and establish a permanent art museum for Nova Scotia. We will always be

The Centennial Art Gallery, Halifax Citadel.

indebted to Commander Law and the many other volunteers for the essential roles they played in developing and nurturing the AGNS through its formative years. Their perseverance was rewarded in March of 1975, when the NSMFA moved into the Anna Leonowens Gallery in the former Nova Scotia College of Art and Design building on Coburg Road, left empty when NSCAD moved to its new downtown home in Historic Properties at Duke and Granville Streets. A retrospective exhibition of paintings by LeRoy Zwicker opened the new gallery space a few months later.

The 1976 *Folk Art of Nova Scotia* exhibition in the main gallery at the Coburg Road site (the former Anna Leonowens Gallery, Nova Scotia College of Art and Design).

At the last annual meeting of the NSMFA, on November 18, 1975, a resolution was proclaimed authorizing the president and treasurer to execute all documents effecting the transfer of the assets of the Museum to the Art Gallery of Nova Scotia. A month later, the Act to establish the Art Gallery of Nova Scotia was proclaimed. The official dedication of the Gallery took place on December 9, 1975. The Honourable Clarence L. Gosse, Lieutenant Governor of Nova Scotia, presided on that occasion and inducted the first Board of Governors of the AGNS, under Robert Manuge as Chairman. Gosse became the Gallery's first honorary patron, a position held by every Lieutenant Governor since that time. The Department of Recreation, responsible for cultural matters under Minister A. Garnet Brown, and succeeding Deputy Ministers Hugh Conrod and Louis Stephen, laid down a vision for cultural development in the province that, over time, would bring about the establishment of many of our now-familiar cultural institutions and programs.

Robert Manuge, first Chair of the AGNS, with The Honourable Gerald Regan, Premier of Nova Scotia; The Honourable Clarence Gosse, Lieutenant Governor of Nova Scotia; and A. Garnet Brown, Minister of the Department of Recreation; Mrs. Gosse, Mrs. Regan, and Mrs. Brown at the ceremony establishing the AGNS in 1975.

The success of any gallery in achieving its objectives depends on the energy, imagination, and resources of its staff, Board of Governors, and always, its volunteers. The act establishing the Gallery set up a Board of Governors of fifteen people, five of whom must be from outside the metropolitan area. The Board, through the years, has included public-spirited individuals who have been generous with their time and expertise. They have given the organization stability, brought the interests of the community to the organization, and represented the interests of the Gallery to the community.

The Gallery's Coburg Road location provided for a modest operation, and allowed the AGNS to conduct research, build its collection, develop travelling exhibitions, establish art education and art conservation programs, and see to the growth of both professional staff and a dedicated core of volunteers. Shortly after the proclamation of the Art Gallery of Nova Scotia, our first education programs were implemented by Education Officer Alice Hoskins, with the primary aim of enabling the public to enjoy a dialogue with a wide variety of visual art and to relate it to daily life. Succeeding curators Kathy Brown, Virginia Stephen, and Dale Sheppard have continued to develop exciting strategies for awakening the aesthetic response of gallery users. Critical to the success of our education programs are the great numbers of volunteer guides who, along with the professional art-education staff, have worked to make the Gallery's education and public programs the finest in the country. As the provincial art gallery, the AGNS has always considered outreach a priority, and shortly after 1975 an active travelling exhibition program was put into place, bringing the collection and temporary exhibitions to galleries and cultural centres throughout Nova Scotia, and later to institutions throughout Atlantic Canada.

The AGNS outreach program begins with the acquisition of a gallery vehicle courtesy of Nova Scotia Tractors and Equipment Limited. The Honourable Greg Kerr, Minister of Culture, looks on with Jack Craig, AGNS Director Bernard Riordon, and travelling exhibitions coordinator Deborah Young.

The Art Sales and Rental Society moved its operations to rooms in the old St. Andrews Hall at the Coburg Road site in 1978. The early 1980s saw a modest expansion in the Coburg Road site with the addition of a gallery shop, a Permanent Collection gallery, additional offices, and collection storage on the second floor. Our first fine art conservator was hired in 1980, and a conservation laboratory established as a modest facility in the basement. By this time, however, it had become evident that the site was too small to accommodate the exhibitions and programming needed to serve the people of the province, and that Dalhousie University had its own need for the space.

LeRoy and Marguerite Zwicker, champions of the arts and the Art Gallery of Nova Scotia

A site on the Halifax Waterfront, adjacent to the Maritime Museum of the Atlantic, was identified as a suitable home for the Gallery in a preliminary design study completed in 1983. LeRoy and Marguerite Zwicker, long-time arts advocates and patrons of the arts, pledged the lead gift toward the building of our first permanent home. The Zwickers' pledge of financial support and the dedicated work of Board, staff, and volunteers provided the incentive and leadership that persuaded the provincial and federal governments to announce joint funding of $4 million to be allocated to the permanent-home project in 1984. A goal of $8 million was set, and local businessman and former Chair of the Board of Governors, Jack Craig, provided the leadership for the capital campaign. In 1985, however, the province offered the Gallery the old Post Office, also known as the Dominion Building, which sat across the street from Province House at Hollis and Cheapside.

Since the time of its construction, the Dominion Building has been a focal point in the political life of Nova Scotia. So strong was anti-Confederation sentiment in Nova Scotia in 1867, that the provincial government initially refused to transfer the Post Office to the new federal government. The exchange was finally arranged in 1871, when Nova Scotia received payment from the federal government for half its construction cost plus interest. The federal government agreed to allow the province the opportunity of finding a suitable function for the historic structure, unoccupied after 1981. On April 30, 1985, the Minister announced that the old Dominion Building would become the new home of the Art Gallery of Nova Scotia. Although it represented a dramatic change in direction, requiring the renovation and conversion of an existing building rather than the erection of a new structure, enthusiasm and momentum were quickly adapted and redirected.

Britannia, sitting atop Gallery North, is a symbol of industry, prosperity, and peace.

Designed by Halifax architect David Stirling, and built by Samuel Brookfield, who oversaw the construction of the harbour defences, the Dominion building, made of warm brown sandstone, was finally completed in late December of 1867. In architectural style it reflects the highly decorative European influences of the time. Originally, a cupola rose from the centre of its pitch roof to an impressive height of 31 metres above the ground, dominating the skyline of old Halifax. Over the years, the interior and exterior features of the building have been altered in accordance with the requirements of its many users and through the effects of climatic conditions, respectively. Peering out from atop the south pediment of the future home of the AGNS was Britannia, a symbol of industry, prosperity, and peace. The

The 1985 Building Fund launched its campaign with the unveiling of the plans for the Gallery's future home in the Dominion Building. In attendance were Jean Marc Pellerine, Federal Department of Communications; Struan Robertson, AGNS Board Chair; The Honourable John Buchanan, Premier of Nova Scotia; Robert Radchuck, Building Fund Vice-Chair; and John R. Craig, Building Fund General Chair.

Dignitaries and guests gather for the official opening of the first permanent home for the Art Gallery of Nova Scotia in its downtown location on November 5, 1988.

figure was adopted as the symbolic matriarch of the AGNS Fund Raising Campaign, and appeared on all related printed material.

The Gallery's Building Committee worked with the architects, Lydon Lynch Associates Limited, and the provincial Department of Government Services, to produce a purpose-built, modern art gallery within the existing structure of a heritage building. The last exhibition at the Coburg Road site, *Select Acquisitions from the Permanent Collection 1975-1987*, celebrated what the Gallery had achieved at its temporary home. On November 5, 1988, "a celebration of homecoming" took place with the official opening of the first permanent home for the Art Gallery of Nova Scotia. The official opening committee, with Alex Colville as Chairman, worked with the Protocol Office and a team of staff and volunteers to ensure participation by people from all over the province in celebrating one of the most important cultural events in the history of Nova Scotia.

Space was designed on the fourth floor of the new building to accommodate a modern conservation lab, with the integrated exhaust systems and wiring required to support the specialized equipment used in the preservation of works of art. Today, the AGNS boasts the only publicly funded conservation lab in the province dedicated to the care of paintings. Over the years, the Department of Canadian Heritage has been generous in providing support for conservation initiatives such as the purchase of new equipment and, more recently, the restoration of the Maud Lewis House.

With thirteen permanent collection rooms, an education gallery, and three temporary exhibition spaces, the AGNS was finally in a position to begin to serve the people of the province properly. The expansion of its various roles, however, led to rapid growth of the Permanent Collection and of education programming, making additional space essential. In 1997, Premier John Savage announced that two-and-a-half floors of the Provincial Building would be available for the Phase II expansion of the AGNS. Made possible through the donation of space by the province and private funding, the capital expansion was provided a lead gift by Barbara and Norman Newman for the establishment of an education centre in their name. The expanded facility opened in June 1998. In addition to the education centre in

Premier John Savage with (L to R) Evan Petley Jones, AGNS Acquisition Chair; AGNS Board Chair Merv Russell; Minister of Education and Culture Robbie Harrison; artist John Greer; and Mrs. Dini, wife of the President of Italy.

Gallery South, the expansion provided for the Scotiabank Maud Lewis Gallery, additional display areas, storage and office space, a gallery shop, a café, and new quarters for the Art Sales and Rental Society. Space freed up in Gallery North allowed for creation of the Nova Scotia College of Art and Design Gallery, the Laufer Family Gallery; and the Anthony and Jane Shaw Law Gallery of Inuit Art.

Mary Maddox and Barbara Newman with The Honourable Robbie Harrison, Minister of Education and Culture, and AGNS Chair Fred Fountain, at the ribbon-cutting ceremony for the opening of the AGNS Phase II expansion.

Since 1997, there have been ongoing efforts to establish a Western Branch of the Art Gallery of Nova Scotia in Yarmouth. The former Royal Bank Building on Main Street and the adjacent property were acquired with a lead gift from the Royal Bank. A capital campaign and a building committee, made up of leaders in the Yarmouth community, have worked diligently with our Board and staff to establish the first AGNS satellite gallery. A grand opening of that facility is anticipated in 2003.

The Western Branch of the Art Gallery of Nova Scotia in Yarmouth, the first satellite gallery of the AGNS.

A Collection to House

The collection inherited from the NSMFA by the AGNS in the mid-1970s was small with many gaps, a result of the random manner in which it had been assembled over the decades. The majority of its 228 works had been donated to the Museum, whose collection grew largely without direction or plan, let alone a comprehensive collections policy. In 1974, with the assistance of the National Museums of Canada and the Nova Scotia Department of Recreation, the Gallery undertook to catalogue all provincially owned works of art. In that year, too, an acquisitions policy was established which placed the responsibility for recommending new acquisitions to the collection on curatorial staff, instead of on the informal decisions of artists and dedicated amateurs. The policy recognizes the Gallery's particular responsibility with respect to the art of Nova Scotia; however, the range of the collection extends beyond Nova Scotia and the Atlantic Provinces to encompass art from across Canada. Policy also allows for the consideration of specialized areas of collecting beyond Canadian art. The priorities for the collection as outlined by that acquisition policy were as follows:

- to acquire important works of art by artists associated with Nova Scotia
- to acquire a significant representation of Canadian art, both historical and contemporary

- to continue to develop an important collection of Nova Scotia folk art and extend it to include significant works from others areas of Canada
- to acquire works of art by international artists in order to extend the range of the collection

In many ways this policy is an outgrowth of the original NSMFA collection, which had developed according to the taste and limited finances of its volunteer membership. Steps have been taken to collect works by following planned objectives, and to encourage an aggressive program of acquisition by gift. That the major areas of collecting have remained constant reflects the longstanding cultural traditions of the province.

Historical Nova Scotian and Canadian Art

Collecting the best available contemporary Nova Scotian and Canadian art, as well as historical paintings, had been a concern of the original NSMFA. Those early works collected by the Museum are now the foundation for our collection of early twentieth-century painting, including works by such outstanding artists as Helen McNichol, Ernest Lawson, Arthur Lismer, Edith Smith, Elizabeth Nutt, Marjorie Tozer, and Stanley Royle. The acquisitions policy of the AGNS has been directed to the continued enrichment of the Gallery's permanent collection of historical and contemporary paintings, sculptures, prints, and drawings, now enhanced by photographs, video, and other new media.

Permanent Collection galleries dedicated to historical Nova Scotian art include the Portrait Gallery and Nova Scotian Painting Gallery sponsored by the City of Halifax, and the gallery for Nova Scotian Art 1900-1975 sponsored by LeRoy and Marguerite Zwicker. Two gallery spaces in Gallery North today bear the names of LeRoy and Marguerite Zwicker, who together made an expansive and defining commitment to art in this province; the Zwicker legacy will be enjoyed by future generations. The AGNS was the residual heir to the Estate of LeRoy and Marguerite Zwicker, whose gift established the AGNS Endowment Fund, and included an important collection of art. As well, the Royal Bank Gallery of Canadian Art and the Christopher Ondaatje Gallery both feature changing exhibitions of works by outstanding Canadian artists.

Contemporary Collection

The definition of contemporary art is ever-changing. For the present purpose, we have considered the move into the Centennial Art Gallery in 1968 as the beginning of the contemporary period, a moment in history that coincides with revolutionary changes at the Nova Scotia College of Art and Design in the late 1960s. The essentially conservative aesthetic governing art in Nova Scotia was catapulted into the front lines of the battles that characterize art of the late twentieth-century. The

Gallery has endeavoured to select works by the most outstanding adherents of the many approaches to art-making in the province since then. Though individual donations have continued to play a dominant role in the growth of the collection, certain programs have allowed the Gallery to make strategic purchases over the years. In 1982, Maritime Tel & Tel began a relationship with the Gallery that created a yearly art-acquisition award. Initially used to provide the cover images for the annual telephone directory, the program continued until 2000 and brought nineteen works by Atlantic Canadian artists into the Permanent Collection. Throughout the life of the AGNS, the Art Sales and Rental Society has continued to play a key role. One thing that has remained constant in the history of the Society, as it moved with us from temporary location to temporary location, is the dedication that its volunteers have brought to the organization. Always instrumental in the development of our Permanent Collection, the Art Sales and Rental Society has contributed greatly to the enhancement of artistic and cultural life in the province. Most recently, the Society has assumed responsibility for the acquisition of *Dog in Car* (1999) by Alex Colville.

Equally important to the AGNS has been The Canada Council for the Arts Acquisition Assistance Program, which provides matching funds for the acquisition of contemporary Canadian art. The support of The Canada Council has been invaluable in the development of our contemporary collection, and in providing essential support and exposure for our artists. The Friends of the AGNS have also been diligent supporters of the Gallery's programs and acquisitions. Their support extends to all levels of the Gallery operation, and makes it possible to provide valuable education and other programs that enhance the on-site experience for the visitors of all ages who come to view these new acquisitions

In 2001, Denis Connor and Harold P. Connor announced their gift toward the establishment of the Elisabeth Connor NSCAD Archive at the AGNS. The Archive will provide a repository to locate and collect important support material representative of faculty and graduates of the Nova Scotia College of Art and Design who have made a significant contribution to Nova Scotia, Canada, and the world through their art practice. At the same time, the creation of a Curator of Contemporary Art position has made possible the expertise to concentrate greater emphasis, in our collection and exhibition practices, in the area of contemporary Canadian Art. Contemporary Nova Scotian and Canadian art is featured in the LeRoy and Marguerite Zwicker Gallery, the City of Dartmouth Gallery, and the Frederick and Elizabeth Fountain Gallery of Contemporary Nova Scotian Art.

First Nations and Inuit Art

The AGNS acquired its first piece of Inuit Art in 1980, and this area of the Permanent Collection has continued to grow since our move into permanent quarters in 1988. The dedication of a new Inuit Gallery is a permanent testimony to the love for the North and its artists developed by Tony Law and his wife Jane Shaw. The AGNS began to collect art by First Nations artists actively in 1993, following its groundbreaking exhibition, *Pe'l A'tukwey: Recent Work by Mi'kmaq and Maliseet Artists.* With the support of The Canada Council in 1999, we were able to appoint a curator of First Nations Art, who then oversaw the establishment of a dedicated gallery space, sponsored by the HRM Millennium Committee and ExxonMobil, in 2001. Our First Nations Gallery allows us to integrate this important aspect of our cultural heritage into ongoing Gallery programming, and to promote a greater understanding of the diverse and rich artistic cultures in Nova Scotia and Canada.

Nova Scotian Folk Art

The 1985 exhibition, *Spirit of Nova Scotia: Traditional Decorative Folk Art 1780-1930,* enabled the Gallery to build on the reputation it had acquired with its seminal 1976 exhibition, *Folk Art of Nova Scotia*, which travelled across Canada to great acclaim. The development of a folk art component has been one of the highlights of AGNS collection growth, a complement to our contemporary and historical fine art holdings, and one celebrating extraordinary creative work by ordinary people. In 1984, the province acquired, for its Gallery, the Maud Lewis House from the Maud Lewis Painted House Society, with a view to displaying it permanently within the AGNS. Folk Art has delighted visitors to the Jack and Joan Craig Gallery since our move into the Dominion Building in 1988, but not until the completion of the Phase II expansion in 1998 did we finally have the necessary space to mount a permanent exhibition of the Maud Lewis House in the Scotiabank Gallery in Gallery South. Conservation of the house, under the direction of Fine Art Conservator Laurie Hamilton, was carried out at a site at Sunnyside Mall in Bedford, and provided a unique opportunity for Nova Scotians to watch a team of conservators at work and to reveal their own memories of the province's foremost folk artist.

Ceramics

In 1996, the Gallery dedicated the Lloyd and Jean Shaw Gallery for Ceramics with a special exhibition, organized by the Nova Scotia Potters Guild, that began with pottery dating from prehistoric times and continued through the nineteenth century to studio and production pieces by Nova Scotia's major potters up to 1970. Since that time, this gallery has installed annual exhibitions featuring pieces from the collection, which includes some of the finest work by historical and contemporary Nova Scotian ceramists. As well, individual works by renowned international artists provide a context in which to view the achievement of these artists.

International Painting and Sculpture

Primarily, the International collection reflects the taste and collecting habits of the citizens of this province, and their generous impulses to support the provincial gallery. Although the NSMFA purchased one painting by a member of the Bassano family, all other examples of international painting and sculpture have come into the collection by donation, unless the artwork has had an obvious importance in the history of the province. During the Gallery's tenancy at the Coburg Road site, four important paintings of early Halifax by the British artist Dominique Serres were acquired that extended the range of the Gallery's collection of historical works of art relating to Nova Scotia back to the founding of Halifax in 1749. The AGNS called on many private sources to collect the funds for this purchase. Since 1984, the Gallery has enjoyed support from the Department of Canadian Heritage, through the Cultural Property Export and Import Act, when such works come on the market, such as the Reynolds portrait of Lord Halifax.

Two gallery spaces are dedicated to the exhibition of the International collection, the Alice Hoskins Gallery for International Art and the Laufer Family Gallery, which usually includes paintings and sculpture gifted by that family to the AGNS. A large donation of Mediaeval and early Renaissance sculpture by the Archdiocese of Halifax now provides context for the small collection of historical European paintings acquired by the NSFMA and the AGNS.

Prints and Drawings

The Prints and Drawings collection crosses the cultural divisions that define other sections of the Permanent Collection, including both historical and contemporary examples of Nova Scotian, Canadian, and International printmaking, watercolour painting, and drawing. Donations of substantial print collections assembled by Harold Giddens, Hugh and Suzanne Conrod, and John and Norma Oyler have made Prints and Drawings the largest section of the Permanent Collection, with over 6,500 individual works. Two annual themed exhibitions are featured in the John and Norma Oyler Gallery of Early Canadian Prints and Drawings, and our corridor galleries draw on Canadiana, European, Oriental, and American prints and drawings for exhibitions.

The Permanent Collection also includes major collections of works on paper by prominent Nova Scotian artists such as Carol Fraser, Nelly Beveridge Gray, J. Frederic McCulloch, Henry Orenstein, and Roger Savage.

As the Gallery's 100th anniversary approaches, in 2008, it is well to look back at the challenges surmounted in the past and to draw strength from them as we confront new economic constraints and cultural challenges. This publication affirms our commitment to the past, the present, and the future. The plant that grew from that seed planted more than nine decades ago flourished briefly, then withered and almost died from time to time, but it clung tenaciously to life. Nurtured by dedicated staff, board members, patrons, volunteers, and visitors, it is now in glorious bloom.

In this age of lifelong learning, art museums need to constantly re-invent themselves to meet the needs of the general public, and to reach out to the community. Reinvention of itself has been the history of the Art Gallery of Nova Scotia. With this publication we present you, the gallery-goer and interested reader, with some of the highlights of our Permanent Collection. Celebrate with us the artistic flowering of this province.

Bernard Riordon, O.C.
Director and CEO, 1973-2002
Art Gallery of Nova Scotia

AGNS education and outreach programs introduce another exciting dimension to the Gallery.

CANADIAN HISTORICAL PAINTING

CANADIAN HISTORICAL PAINTING

The collection mandate of the Art Gallery of Nova Scotia recognizes our cultural heritage as Canadians and our identity as Nova Scotians as underlying principles, with a parallel commitment to the acquisition of contemporary art by purchase and, more frequently, by needful donation from artists, members, and supporters. The same principles operated implicitly in the small collection previously acquired by the Nova Scotia Museum of Fine Arts, whose carefully considered purchases of contemporary art decades ago now enhance that heritage and identity. The art of Nova Scotia is naturally its primary concern, but the AGNS has endeavoured to develop a representation of Canadian art to provide a context within which to view the accomplishments of Nova Scotian artists.

Throughout the eighteenth century, British and occasionally European artists visited this province and other areas of the country; not until the early nineteenth century, however, did Nova Scotian and Canadian artists begin to create the works that now define our identity. The first native-born Nova Scotian artist of note, Joseph Brown Comingo (see Fig. 105), painted miniature portraits and topographical views, in watercolour only, during the second decade of the century. His premature death in 1821 from yellow fever, while sketching the seacoast around Nassau on commission from the British government, cut short a promising career. Comingo was succeeded by the Cumbrian-born William Valentine, who immigrated to Nova Scotia in 1818 and perfected his craft as a portrait painter in Halifax. Stretching across three decades, his practice extended throughout the Atlantic Provinces. The nine portraits in the AGNS collection, such as that of *Mrs. Grace Langford Nordbeck* (Fig. 1), document a prosperous and self-assured middle class with a taste for naturalistic representation in a plain style that contrasted with grander portraits in Europe. The collection also includes work by the painter and printmaker John Stevenet Clow, who worked in partnership with Valentine from time to time, and by Cornelius Krieghoff, the Amsterdam-born artist, who was memorializing the habitants of Lower Canada in his paintings at this period. William Harris Jones, an art teacher in Halifax, organized the first art exhibitions in Canada in 1830 and 1831. *Cattle at a Watering Place*, shown in the 1831 exhibition by Henry Samuel Davis, an officer in the 52nd Oxfordshire Light Infantry, may be related to Davis' 1832 painting in the AGNS collection known as *An Evening View of Halifax*. Stationed in Halifax for less than four years, however, Davis can not be considered a Nova Scotian painter.

Two more Nova Scotian artists emerged at mid-century, the marine painter John O'Brien, and the illustrator and landscape artist Robert Wilkie. The latter immigrated to Boston and pursued his career in the United States, but O'Brien reached unprecedented heights in his field until eye damage, caused by the mercury fumes met in his 'other' job in a photography studio, curtailed his career. O'Brien's 1856 portrait of *The Arab, Brigantine, and the Milo, Brig, off Halifax Harbour* (Fig. 2), the gift of Mr. and Mrs. Alex Doyle, reveals his superb command of graduated space and diffused light. The Gallery's collection of nine O'Brien paintings began with a gift from the painter and ceramist Alice Egan Hagen, of three paintings of the Galatea in 1955. Valentine's contemporary, the Prussian-born William Raphael, renowned for his genre scenes such as *The Old Pedlar* (Fig. 3), settled in Montreal in 1857. Though Raphael supported his art-making by colouring photographs for William Notman, and by producing anatomical drawings for Sir William Osler, he avoided eye damage and later became a charter member of the Royal Canadian Academy.

The next generation of artists in Nova Scotia included two more British immigrants, George Harvey and Forshaw Day. Harvey served as first Headmaster of the newly established Victoria School of Art and Design in 1887; Day (another charter member of the RCA) had already left Nova Scotia to take up a post as drawing master at the Royal Military College in Kingston. Harvey's meticulously rendered *Welsh Courtyard* (Fig. 4) may be compared with landscapes in the collection by Thomas Mower Martin and Homer Watson, the latter artist designated "the Canadian Constable" by Oscar Wilde in 1882. The work of these three artists stands in marked contrast to that of Frances Jones, who has been elsewhere acknowledged as the first Canadian artist to introduce Impressionist techniques into her paintings. Although she studied in the relatively conservative Paris studio of Auguste Feyen-Perrin, the Halifax-born Jones had obviously paid close attention to floral still lifes shown in the Impressionist exhibitions by Monet and Van Gogh before she painted her *Vase of Peonies* (Fig. 5) in 1882.

It was perhaps their familiarity with Jones' work that motivated the first purchase decision reached by the fledgling NSMFA in November of 1909. The decision to purchase a Helen Galloway McNicoll painting was followed immediately by a public appeal for funds, establishing a tradition familiar to Gallery members today. With the purchase of *Midsummer* (Fig. 8), the NSMFA became the first art museum in Canada to acquire a painting by an artist now widely recognized for her contribution to Canadian Impressionism. Ten years later, the NSMFA organized an exhibition of Impressionist paintings by the expatriate Nova Scotian, Ernest Lawson. Their purchase of six paintings from that exhibition, including *The Bridge* (Fig. 9), formed the basis for the AGNS collection of ten Lawson paintings today, the largest in Canada. Lawson's spiky impasto technique, which emerges, as New York critic F.K. Price famously observed, from "...a palette of crushed jewels," contrasts with the lavishly applied swatches of luminous colour that characterize work by the expatriate Canadian painter James Wilson Morrice, whose *Parisian Street Scene* (Fig. 7) is one of four small paintings in the collection, the gift of Eleanore Morrice. Morrice began his career heavily indebted to James McNeill Whistler, and Henry Mortikar Rosenberg, principal of the VSAD (the fifth) between 1898 and 1910, shares that allegiance to both Whistler and the Impressionists. Many of his paintings of Halifax harbour and the Dartmouth lakes convey a sense of the Impressionists, but *Two Girls* (Fig. 6), the painting he gifted to the NSMFA during World War I, suggests his indebtedness to his earlier master.

Lacking its own building, the NSMFA originally housed its collection at the art school. As VSAD's principal between 1916 and 1919, Arthur Lismer served as custodian of the collection. The influence of McNicoll's painting on his own approach to painting leaps out in a comparison of the two works purchased by the NSMFA from his exhibition in 1919, *Sunglow*, 1915 and *Sackville River,* 1917 (Fig. 10). The precise brushstrokes of the decorative *Sunglow*, a picture of his friend Tom Thomson canoeing against a curtain of autumn colours in Algonquin Park, has been replaced by the bold brushwork of *Sackville River*. It was that new freedom of expression that Lismer carried back to Ontario, where he became a founding member of the Group of Seven in 1920. The small Group of Seven collection at the AGNS gives special weight to its members who painted in this province, such as J.E.H. MacDonald, who often painted with his close friend Lewis Smith at Petite Rivière (Fig. 11). A.Y. Jackson's *Entrance to Halifax Harbour* is held by the Tate Gallery, but our own collection is graced by Lauder Brunton's gift of *Little Fox River, Gaspé* (Fig. 19), whose snow-flattened fields and swirling shadows produce a rolling, linear rhythm that energizes the entire canvas.

The rhythms of the land inspired the Group of Seven in central Canada; those of the sea inform the work of Nova Scotian artists who developed their own consistent regional voice in the years following Lismer's departure. Lismer was replaced at the art school by Elizabeth Styring Nutt (like him, a graduate of the art school in Sheffield), who continued to serve as curator of the collection, and who changed the name of the school to the Nova Scotia College of Art in 1924. Parallel, but distinct from the Group of Seven, a Nova Scotia landscape school developed during the 1920s out of the North American Impressionist heritage and British Impressionism, as filtered through Sheffield, and was furthered by the arrival from that school of Stanley Royle in 1932. Such paintings as Nutt's *Winter, Northwest Arm, Halifax* (Fig. 12), Marjorie Tozer's *Windswept* (Fig. 13), Edith Smith's *"The Rum Runner" at Lunenburg* (Fig.14), Mabel Killam Day's *Fishing Houses* (Fig. 15), and Royle's *Coastal Rocks/The Stillness of Dawn* reveal this dual inheritance. Royle was also a brilliant and sensitive portraitist. For his portrait of *John Keeling* (Fig. 17), who probably sat for a Life Class at the NSCA, Royle chose the profile format used by Piero della Francesca for *Federigo da Montefeltro*, perhaps motivated by the partial blindness afflicting both sitters. Royle retained the portrait in his personal collection when he returned to England following World War II. A grant from the Cultural Property Export Review Board enabled the AGNS to purchase the portrait in 1992. The influence of Montreal's Beaver Hall Group touches another portrait, that of *The Soldier's Wife* (Fig. 20) by Yarmouth artist Elizabeth Cann, who studied in Montreal in 1929. Cann's painting was one of fifteen works in the Diploma Collection of the Nova Scotia Society of Artists deeded to the Gallery in 1974. Another stunning portrait from this period is *Seated Nude* (Fig. 16), painted by NSCA graduate J. Frederic McCulloch, who captures the Olympic detachment of his sitter in a composition reminiscent of Whistler's *Arrangement in Black and Grey, Nº 2*, the portrait of Carlyle. The artist's widow, Alice McCulloch Sutton, has generously gifted the AGNS with forty-four paintings and drawings that survey his career in Europe.

The Canadian art world achieved an unprecedented degree of unity in 1940 with the appearance of *Maritime Art*, the first art magazine in the country. Promoted by the artists LeRoy and Marguerite Zwicker and the critic Walter Abell, and published by the Maritime Art Association, the journal was moved to Ontario in 1943 and became *Canadian Art*.

Canada was slow to embrace abstraction wholeheartedly, but, in spite of a traditional predisposition toward landscape, artists were increasingly less interested in representing the naturalistic world than in presenting their particular vision of the world on canvas. David Milne considered his paintings to be "adventures in shape, colour, texture, and space," as evidenced in *House and Clouds* (Fig. 18). In Halifax, LeRoy Zwicker had absorbed the lessons of the previous century in his Cézanne-derived *Blue Hills of Maine*, 1950, and was soon producing totally abstract canvases such as *Abstract* (Fig. 23). At the same time, the Montreal artist Anne Savage was combining landscape with an abstract exploration of colour and rhythm, as in *Sundance Canyon* (Fig. 22), another gift of Lauder Brunton. Wilderness landscape gave way, as well, to social themes among a small but important circle of Canadian postwar artists. Trained at the Art Students' League in New York, Henry Orenstein brought to Social Realism his own response to paintings in the Cubist and Expressionist styles which he had seen while a soldier overseas. His *Self-portrait of a Fur Worker* (Fig. 21) conveys the concentration required of a worker in the garment trade, acknowledges his dependence on others engaged in simultaneous tasks, and elevates them all to a dignity transcending Toronto's Spadina sweatshops.

During the 1950s, artists in Nova Scotia approached painting as both a representational and abstract, if not yet nonfigurative, art. Reacting to the new aesthetic, Marion Bond, who had earlier painted many landscapes and portraits now in the AGNS collection, adopted the vocabulary of analytical Cubism for her 1957 interpretation of *Halifax Harbour* (Fig. 24). At the same time, paintings such as *On the Deck of the Ship Torrens* (Fig. 25) by Jack Gray, the gift of Dr. Hugh Smythe, refer back to the long-established tradition of marine painting. By the end of the decade, however, abstraction had become the dominant aesthetic in Canadian painting. The AGNS collection is able to represent this national shift with such works as Harold Town's *Night Riders,* and *Composition* (Fig. 26), a black-and-white painting by Paul-Émile Borduas, painted in Paris near the end of his life. Considered the greatest Canadian painter of the post-war era by most critics, Borduas attempted to paint the non-material world of emotions and sensations. When he issued *Refus global* in 1948, attacking the conformism and traditionalism of Québec, Borduas had hoped that the constraints hindering individual and collective creativity would be broken. His disillusionment a decade later is reflected in the starkness of his final canvases. Borduas' painting is one of the highlights of a collection of Canadian art gifted to the AGNS by Christopher Ondaatje in 1994. One Canadian artist who remained resolutely grounded in reality rather than abstraction was Fredericton-native Goodridge Roberts. Three still lifes in the collection, dating from 1927 to 1965 (Fig. 28), reveal his skill as a colourist from the beginning, as well as the vibrant colour palette that characterized his later works.

Nova Scotians have never acceded blindly to the cultural dominance of Canada, so painters here continued to explore both figurative and abstract approaches to art-making during a decade when Painters 11 in Toronto, the Regina 5 in the West, and the Automatistes in Québec committed totally to abstraction. Alex Colville's *Ocean Limited* (Fig. 27), (the name of the train that once ran regularly between Halifax and Montreal), presents its own challenge to critics who would insist that representation has no place in modern art, for it is as rigorously conceived as work by the most abstract theorist. It is not a picture of the everyday world but an intellectual intervention with the world in which the artist has chosen to live. Colville served as a judge for the *Centennial Exhibitions* that inaugurated the new exhibition space established by the NSMFA on Citadel Hill in 1967. The Province of Nova Scotia selected a Centennial Collection of twenty-two paintings from these exhibitions as a gift to the NSMFA. Half of these, works such as *Blue Mosque* by Ruth Wainwright, represent a balance between the figurative and the abstract. The Canadian landscape tradition inherited from the Group of Seven informs Tony Law's *Nova Scotia's Rugged Coast* (Fig. 29), among the others.

Taken as a whole, the Centennial Collection serves as a symbol for the state of art-making in the province at an important moment in history. The country's

1967 centenary had been celebrated by the establishment of a provincial exhibition space that would soon grow into the Art Gallery of Nova Scotia. In that same year, Garry Neill Kennedy was appointed president of the Nova Scotia College of Art, and the direction of art being made in Nova Scotia would soon take a radical turn.

Mora Dianne O'Neill
Associate Curator Historical Prints and Drawings

FIGURE. 1
William Valentine
(1798 - 1849)
Mrs. Grace Langford Nordbeck, c.1830
Oil on canvas, 40.1 x 49.6 cm
Purchased 1980
1980.5

FIGURE. 2
John O'Brien
(1831 - 1891)
The ARAB, *Brigantine, and* MILO, *Brig, off Halifax Harbour,* 1856
Oil on canvas, 58.5 x 78.9 cm
Gift of Judith A. and Alex W. Doyle, Sidney, British Columbia, 1999
1999.272

FIGURE. 3
William Raphael
(1833 - 1924)
The Old Pedlar, 1859
Oil on canvas, 76.3 x 89.1 cm
Acquired from Lawrence W.B. Morris, 1930
1930.2

FIGURE. 4
George Harvey
(1846 - 1910)
Welsh Courtyard (*The Old Farm*), 1875
Oil on canvas, 34.6 x 61.0 cm
Gift of Dr. Eliza Ritchie, Halifax, Nova Scotia, 1919
1933.6

FIGURE. 5
Frances Jones (Bannerman)
(1855 - 1944)
Vase of Peonies, 1882
Oil on canvas, 65.2 x 54.5
Gift of the Family of the Hon. A.G. Jones, Halifax, Nova Scotia, 1933
1933.3

FIGURE. 6
Henry Mortikar Rosenberg
(1858 - 1947)
Two Girls (Two Sisters), c.1897
Oil on canvas, 101.9 x 61.4 cm
Gift of the artist, 1915
1929.4

FIGURE. 7
James Wilson Morrice
(1865 - 1924)
Parisian Street Scene, 1898/9
Oil on panel, 15.4 x 12.3 cm
Gift of the Estate of Miss F. Eleanore Morrice, Montréal, Québec, 1981
1981.11

FIGURE. 8
Helen Galloway McNicoll
(1879 - 1915)
Midsummer (*Farmyard in Brittany; October Morning; Daydreams*), c.1909
Oil on canvas, 61.8 x 72.2 cm
Purchased, 1911
1925.3

FIGURE. 9
Ernest Lawson
(1873 - 1939)
The Bridge, 1912
Oil on canvas, 63.5 x 76.4
Purchased, 1919
1917.3

FIGURE. 10
Arthur Lismer
(1885 - 1969)
Sackville River, 1917
Oil on canvas, 77.2 x 92.4 cm
Purchased, 1919
1925.2

FIGURE. 11
J.E.H. MacDonald
(1873 - 1932)
The Old Dock, Petite Rivière, 1922
Oil on board, 21.4 x 26.4 cm
Purchased, 1994
1994.199

FIGURE. 12
Elizabeth Styring Nutt
(1870 - 1946)
Winter, Northwest Arm, Halifax, 1927
Oil on canvas, 63.6 x 76.1 cm
Gift of Robert L. Stanfield, Ottawa, Ontario,
in memory of Mary Hall Stanfield, 1979
1979.8

FIGURE. 13
Marjorie Hughson Tozer (Leefe)
(1900 - 1959)
Windswept, c.1927
Oil on canvas, 76.7 x 91.7 cm
Purchased, 1938
1938.1

FIGURE. 14
Edith Agnes Smith
(1867 - 1954)
"The Rum Runner" at Lunenburg, 1930
Oil on canvas, 76.8 x 63.8 cm
Gift of the Estate of Edith A. Smith, Halifax, Nova Scotia, 1955
1955.3

FIGURE. 15
Mabel Killam Day
(1884 - 1960)
Fishing Houses, c.1930
Oil on canvas, 91.5 x 68.8 cm
Gift of Tim Margolian, Halifax, Nova Scotia, 1993
1993.96

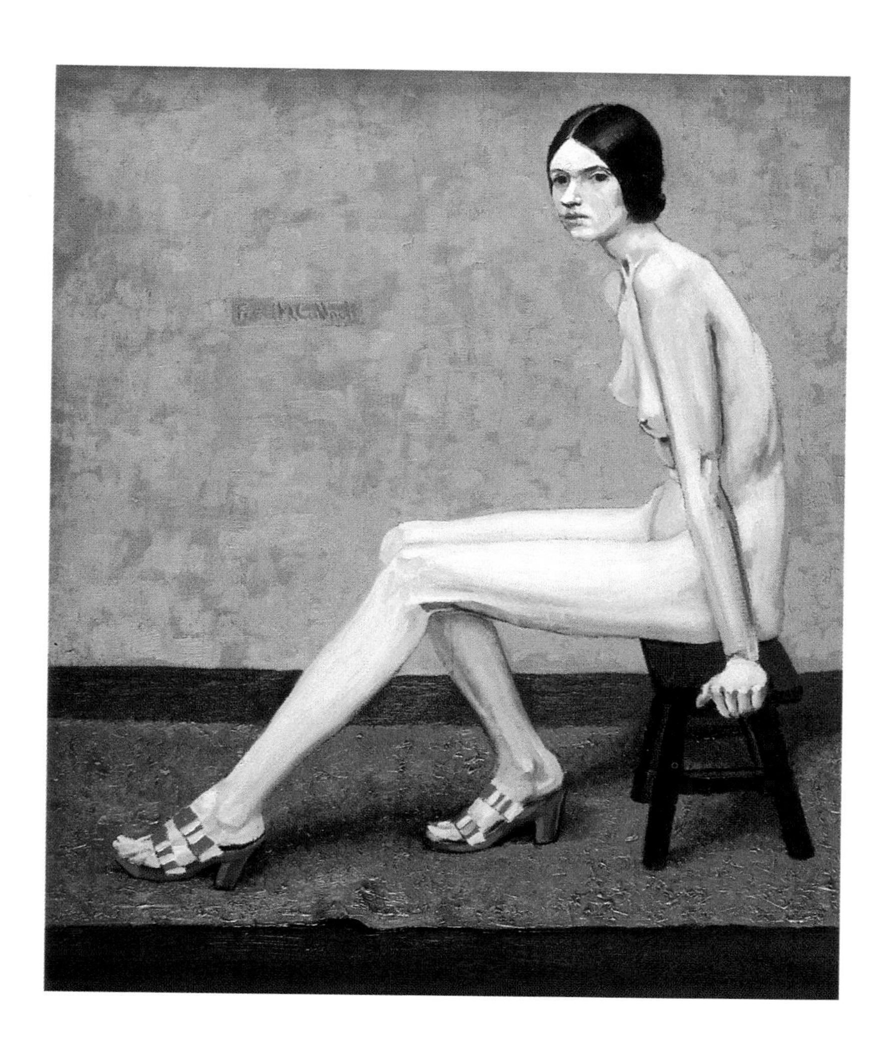

FIGURE. 16
J. Frederic McCulloch
(1905 - 1932)
Seated Nude, 1930
Oil on canvas, 61.0 x 51.0 cm
Gift of Alice McCulloch Sutton, Markham, Ontario, 2000
2000.121

FIGURE. 17
Stanley Royle
(1888 - 1961)
John Keeling, 1932
Oil on canvas, 61.0 x 51.0 cm
Purchased with funds provided by the Government of Canada
under the terms of the Cultural Property Export and Import Act,
the Maritime Life Assurance Company, Senator Donald W. Oliver, QC,
and E. Anthony Ross, 1992
1992.4

FIGURE. 18
David Milne
(1882 - 1953)
House and Clouds, c.1932
Oil on canvas, 51.3 x 61.3 cm
Gift of the Estate of Mrs J.P. Barwick, Ottawa, Ontario,
from the Douglas M. Duncan Collection, 1985
1985.4

FIGURE. 19
A.Y. Jackson
(1882 - 1973)
Little Fox River, Gaspé, 1936
Oil on canvas, 53.5 x 66.5 cm
Gift of Marjorie and Lauder Brunton, Guysborough, Nova Scotia, 1993
1993.102

FIGURE. 20
Elizabeth Lovitt Cann
(1901 - 1977)
The Soldier's Wife, 1941
Oil on canvas, 65.0 x 46.1 cm
Gift of the Nova Scotia Society of Artists, Diploma Collection, 1974
1974.19

FIGURE. 21
Henry Orenstein
(b. 1918)
Self-portrait of a Fur Worker, 1949
Oil on canvas, 98.5 x 71.0 cm
Purchased, 1988
1988.35

FIGURE. 22
Anne Savage
(1896 - 1971)
Sundance Canyon, c.1950
Oil on canvas, 76.5 x 59.5 cm
Gift of Lauder Brunton, in memory of his wife Marjorie,
Guysborough, Nova Scotia, 1999
1999.247

FIGURE. 23
LeRoy Judson Zwicker
(1906 - 1987)
Abstract, n.d.
Oil on canvas 102.0 x 65.8 cm
Gift of the Artist, Halifax, Nova Scotia, 1987
1987.29

FIGURE. 24
Marion Bond
(1900 - 1969)
Halifax Harbour, 1957
Oil on masonite, 77.0 x 92.2 cm
Gift of Marguerite and LeRoy J. Zwicker,
Halifax, Nova Scotia, 1977
1977.41

FIGURE. 25
Jack Gray
(1927 - 1981)
On the Deck of the Ship TORRENS, n.d
Oil on canvas, 91.5 x 52.0 cm
Gift of Dr. Hugh Smythe, Toronto, Ontario, 1982
1982.7

FIGURE. 26
Paul-Émile Borduas
(1905-1960)
Composition, 1959
Oil on canvas, 73.0 x 59.5 cm
Gift of Christopher Ondaatje, Toronto, Ontario, 1994
1994.244

FIGURE. 27
Alex Colville
(b. 1920)
Ocean Limited, 1962
Oil and synthetic resin on board, 68.5 x 119.3 cm
Purchased with funds provided by Christopher Ondaatje, Toronto, Ontario,
the Art Sales and Rental Society, Halifax, Nova Scotia, and a Private Donor, 1994
1994.18

FIGURE. 28
William Goodridge Roberts
(1904 - 1974)
Fruit and Flowers on Blue Cloth, 1965
Oil on canvas, 51.4 x 61.0 cm
Gift of Reuben M. Abramowsky, Montréal, Quebéc, 1988
SC1988.2

FIGURE. 29
C. Anthony Law
(1916 - 1996)
Nova Scotia's Rugged Coast, 1966
Oil on canvas, 91.6 x 101.6 cm
Purchased by Province of Nova Scotia as part of
the Centennial Collection of the Nova Scotia Society of Artists, 1967
1967.9

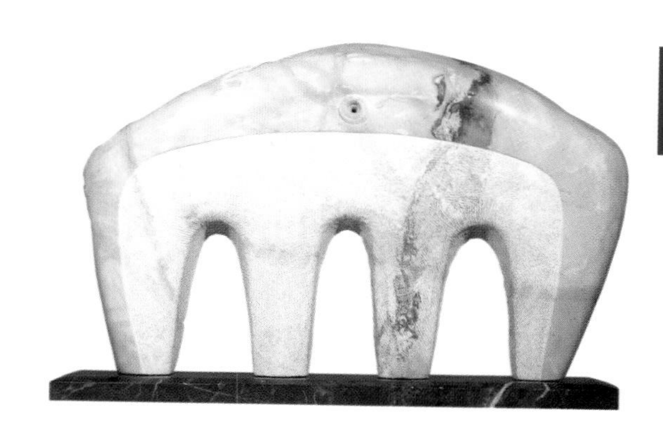

CONTEMPORARY ART

THE CONTEMPORARY COLLECTION
(since 1967)

The Permanent Collection of the Art Gallery of Nova Scotia is, in many respects, a microcosm of the province it reflects. Like Nova Scotia itself, the Contemporary Collection is marked by a rural/urban dichotomy, with Halifax on one side and the rest of the province on the other. Like Nova Scotia, our collection looks to the rest of Canada, and abroad, for inspiration and influence, all the while remaining stubbornly true to this place and this time (whatever time that may be). Our collection mixes tradition and innovation, emotion and cool intellectualism (both pursued with equal passion), and just enough of the best from the rest of the country to put Nova Scotia's best all the more clearly in context.

The Contemporary Collection begins with 1967, Canada's Centennial year, an anniversary that was of key importance to the arts in Nova Scotia. There is no set rule of thumb to determine the cut-off between "historical" and "contemporary"—rather, there are many different habits and conventions. For the purposes of this publication, it was decided that the key date would be the year that the Centennial Art Gallery was established in a powder magazine on Halifax's landmark Citadel Hill (an eighteenth-century British fort). The works on display were from the collection of the Nova Scotia Museum of Fine Arts, a collecting society that had been founded in 1905. Both institutions, the NSMFA and the Centennial Gallery, were the precursors to the present-day AGNS, and it seems appropriate to take the first instance of our putting down roots as the jump-off point for considering the contemporary aspect of the Permanent Collection.

The 1960s were a time of turmoil, and no year was as tumultuous as 1968, the Gallery's first full year of operation. There were student barricades in Paris, assassinations and race riots in the United States, the bloody ending of the "Prague Spring" student riots in Mexico, and more. In art, change was the buzzword, with Pop and Minimalism knocking Abstract Expressionism from its previous pedestal, and with Conceptual Art waiting in the wings. The centre of the art world was firmly set in New York, with the "School of Paris" supplanted by the "New York School" as the model for artists around the world.

Canadian art in this period was undergoing the same sort of strain, with giants such as Jean-Paul Riopelle (Fig. 31) and Jean Paul Lemieux (Fig. 33) eschewing the cool new ideas from New York in favour of their own brand of internationalism. As a relatively new institutional player on the scene, the Art Gallery of Nova Scotia (as it was incorporated in 1975) was not in a good position to acquire a large collection of works by established Canadian and international artists, such as Riopelle and Lemieux. Instead, the decision was taken to focus on the production of the artists of this province as our primary mandate, but with the hopes of acquiring, through purchase and donation, a few key pieces that would help establish a context for the Nova Scotia works in the collection.

The AGNS permanent collection was shaped by the historical events of this region. Feminism was changing the way that art was made and shown, and here in Atlantic Canada an "Acadian Renaissance" was bringing a new generation of Acadian artists to public and critical attention. Yvon Gallant is a central figure in that movement, and *Dit Anne* (Fig. 34) shows him at his whimsical best.

Perhaps no one event more defined, or re-defined art here than the shift of the Nova Scotia College of Art from a smallish, rather traditional institution, to the internationally renowned art school that it is today. In 1968, a new broom swept into the Nova Scotia College of Art (re-named the Nova Scotia College of Art and Design in 1969), in the person of a new president, a 31-year-old Canadian artist named Garry Neill Kennedy.

Kennedy, and the many new faculty members that he brought to Halifax, had very different ideas about art from the rather conservative modernists who had preceded them at NSCAD. These two strains, a radical internationalism and a regional modernism, for want of better terms, would constitute "two solitudes," until a later generation of artists, and a new understanding of the modern, eventually bridged the gap.

In Nova Scotia, as in Canada, the notion of what was contemporary was seemingly decided somewhere far away. In the late '60s, that somewhere was New York, and the revitalized NSCAD became a conduit by which New York ideas such as Conceptual and Minimal Art became the foundation of much new art in Nova Scotia. NSCAD faculty members Jerry Ferguson (Fig. 50), Ron Shuebrook (Fig. 35), Eric Cameron (Fig. 36), and Kennedy himself (Fig. 32), were making paintings that seemed to be about anything but painting, or perhaps about nothing but painting. These artists worked to expunge any trace of emotionalism from their work, using rules-based and serial practices that were the hallmarks of the burgeoning Conceptual Art movement. All of these artists have had a lasting impact on generations of students. The influence of Ferguson, in particular, has been deeply felt in Nova Scotia and beyond. New Brunswick's Gerard Collins (Fig. 49) has pushed the merger of Conceptual ideas and painterly passion in his various series: the *Quodlibet* paintings, the *Work Ethic* paintings, the *Harlequin Romance Series,* the *Beautiful New Brunswick* paintings, and others. The works of Cliff Eyland, Monica Tap (Fig. 58), Jane Mothersell, and Alex Livingston (Fig. 41) all, in various ways, suggest that there is a common interest, in many NSCAD graduates, in combining the intellectual rigour of Conceptualism and the traditions of painting.

However, there is no one "school" of painting in Nova Scotia, and our collection represents a broad spectrum of approaches to this medium. Annapolis Royal's Wayne Boucher is a long-time advocate of abstraction. His painting, *Blue* (Fig. 52), recently acquired as a donation from the artist, is a fine example of Boucher's approach to colour and his insistence on balancing formalism and Expressionism in his work. *Kristallnacht* (Fig. 47), by Nyna Cropas of Clementsport, also reflects the influence of Expressionism, here in a powerful mediation on the horror of the Holocaust. These artists, as well as Susan Feindel, Leya Evelyn, George Walford, Chrystal Clements, Marilyn MacAvoy, Richard Mueller, Suzanne Gauthier, and others, all help tell some of the myriad stories of art in Nova Scotia.

However, while change was taking place at NSCAD, other forces were at work in Nova Scotia. Ruth Wainwright continued her long career as an artist and teacher, exploring her interest in landscape and abstraction well into her eighties (Fig. 39). Alex Colville moved to Wolfville in the 1970s, and his influence on the style most often called "Atlantic Realism" was profound. Tom Forrestall (Fig. 46), Mary Pratt (Fig. 53), and Christopher Pratt (Fig. 45) were all his students, though each brought something new and exciting to their painting. Mary Pratt was once famously called "the visual poet of the kitchen" (by Toronto critic Robert Fulford). *Sunday Dinner,* a large painting of an uncooked roast on a platter, harks back to Dutch still life, as it makes a contemporary statement about women's lives. The quotidian events of a woman's life have always been Mary Pratt's subject matter, a feminist approach that critics and curators are finally acknowledging.

John Nesbitt moved from New York to Cape Breton, bringing with him his high-modernist, Pop-flavoured metal abstraction. *Joetoebloo* (Fig. 38) was acquired from his 1983 exhibition at the AGNS. A key figure in the Nova Scotia scene in the '60s and '70s was Carol Fraser (Fig. 40), a painter and writer who helped foster a community of women artists in Nova Scotia. One of Canada's oldest artist-run centres, Eye Level Gallery, began as a collective of female artists, including one of Fraser's peers, Charlotte Wilson Hammond (Fig. 37). Erica Rutherford arrived in Prince Edward Island in the 1970s, bringing her own distinctive sensibility, and her unique approach to gender issues. Her *Self-portrait in Yellow Stockings* (Fig. 30) is an image of a man considering becoming a woman. Rutherford underwent a sex change in the 1970s, and her work of that period is a very early exploration of the kind of issues about gender that have come to be a hallmark of postmodernism.

Throughout the '70s and '80s, feminism continued to grow as a force in Nova Scotia, as it did almost everywhere in the Western world. One of its biggest influences on the arts was the breaking down of barriers between so-called "high" and "domestic" art. Dartmouth artist Dawn MacNutt combined traditional crafts—in her case weaving and basket making—with sculpture in works such as *Timeless Form*

#V (Fig. 54). NSCAD professor Nancy Edell, who settled in Nova Scotia in the early '80s, has also used domestic crafts in her work. Her hooked-rug works such as *Waiting* (Fig. 42) were an example to a new generation of creators who were pushing at the old hierarchical barriers between the arts.

David Askevold, an early pioneer in video art, and one of the key figures at NSCAD in the '70s and '80s, has gone on to make digital art, remaining at the forefront of innovation (Fig. 57). John Greer, Robin Peck, Dennis Gill, Glen MacKinnon, Thierry Delva, and others were influential in turning Halifax into one of Canada's hotbeds of sculpture. In the 1980s, Greer's work shifted from non-traditional materials and processes to large-scale bronze casting and stone carving. *Temple of the Order of Chaos* (Fig. 44) was made on his first trip to Pietrasantra, Italy, the region where Cararra marble (Michelangelo's material of choice) is still quarried. A later version of this theme, *Origins,* was installed in Ondaatje Court at the AGNS in 1993, after a national competition.

Sculpture remains a medium of central importance in contemporary Nova Scotian art. Alexander Graham, Cal Lane, David Diviney, and Greg Forrest (Fig. 56), among others, have been creating works that some critics have styled "Halifax Sculpture." Forrest's *Algoma* is a sardonic take on Canadian art history. This work, seemingly a mixture of a bicycle and a modernist sculpture from the school of Britain's Anthony Caro, also references the landscape painting of the Group of Seven. Algoma is a part of the Northern Ontario often painted by Group members, and Forrest's sculpture includes several references to the landscape: the blue water bottles that stand in for lakes; the orange ribbon that suggests a sunset; the eponymous "Forrest" that is at once a signature, a fake corporate "logo," and a description of the Canadian shield.

Halifax native Colleen Wolstenholme studied both sculpture and jewelry at NSCAD, and has often used needlework in her art as well. *Xanax 2mg* (Fig. 55) is made of carved hydrocal plaster and was part of a sizeable series of large-scale "pill" sculptures. Wolstenholme, like Forrest, references high modernism as a starting point to create works with both humour and candour. Rebecca Fisk combines found objects with photography in her work about identity, *Confessions of an Invisible Sister* (Fig. 59), about growing up Black in rural Nova Scotia. The panty hose that cover her 4th-grade photo run the available gamut between white and black, as if the young Fisk was trying on each possible shade.

The collecting mandate of AGNS focuses on the art of Nova Scotia, but it obviously remains important to have works by artists from other parts of Canada to help create a context for that collection. The AGNS holds a large collection of paintings of the Nova Scotia landscape, for instance, so a western scene such as Ivan Eyre's *Mountain Meadow* (Fig. 48) is important for balance. Our sculpture collection, too, features work from outside the Atlantic region, and a piece such as Joe Fafard's *John Diefenbaker* (Fig. 43) represents a very different approach from that of such sculptors as Greer, Delva, or MacKinnon.

The contemporary art in the Permanent Collection includes works on paper, paintings, sculptures, photographs, and more. There are areas that we are currently expanding, such as photography and video. Our holdings include photographs by Robert Bean, Susan McEachern, Ronald Caplan, Alvin Comiter, Gary Wilson (Fig. 51), and David Askevold, but as is so often the case, the amount of work worthy of being collected far exceeds our ability to do so. Of course, this can be said of all mediums. Nova Scotia is a dynamic artistic milieu, and the artists in the province are engaged in an unfolding story.

The Permanent Collection has grown partly through purchase, but more and more through donations, which account for the bulk of new acquisitions. The AGNS has had several key donors of contemporary art over the years, including Dr. Lauder Brunton, a former chair of our acquisition committee, as well as Gerald Ferguson, Christopher Ondaatje, Alex Colville, and many others. Our purchase program has been supported by The Canada Council for the Arts, by the Art Sales and Rental Society (supporting the AGNS), by the Friends of the AGNS, by MTT Telecom, and by many other individual, corporate and institutional supporters. All have helped ensure that Nova Scotia's artistic story is available for everyone to experience. Nova Scotia's artists constitute one of our great treasures, and the AGNS Permanent Collection is their monument—a living collection. Over time, it will continue to be available to Nova Scotians and to visitors, so that our stories remain long after the initial telling.

Ray Cronin
Curator of Contemporary Art

FIGURE. 30
Erica Rutherford
(b. 1923)
Self Portrait with Yellow Stockings, 1971
Acrylic on canvas, 126.8 x 122.0 cm
Purchase, 1987
1987.31

FIGURE. 31
Jean-Paul Riopelle
(1923 - 2002)
Fonte des Neiges, 1973
Oil on canvas, 162.5 x 96.5 cm
Purchased with the assistance of the Canada Council Art Bank
Special Purchase Assistance Program, Ottawa, Ontario, 1982
1982.8

FIGURE. 32
Garry Neill Kennedy
(b. 1935)
Untitled, 1975
Acrylic on canvas on plywood, 91.8 x 91.8 cm
Gift of the Artist, Northwest Cove, Nova Scotia, 2000
2000.60

FIGURE. 33
Jean Paul Lemieux
(1904 - 1990)
Le Découvreur, 1976
Oil on canvas, 74.7 x 206 cm
Gift of Christopher Ondaatje, Toronto, Ontario, 1994
1994.246

FIGURE. 34
Yvon Gallant
(b. 1950)
Dit Anne, 1977
Oil on canvas, 173.5 x 173.0 cm
Purchased with the assistance of the Canada Council Art Bank
Special Purchase Assistance Program, Ottawa, Ontario, 1981
1981.44

FIGURE. 35
Ron Shuebrook
(b. 1943)
Untitled (Yellow Field), 1978
Acrylic on canvas, 215.5 x 121.4 cm
Purchase, 1987
1987.36

FIGURE. 36
Eric Cameron
(b. 1935)
Danish Pastry, 1979
Acrylic gesso and acrylic (5,040 half coats) on danish pastry,
21.5 x 33.0 x 32.0 cm
Purchased with the support of the Canada Council
Acquisition Assistance Program, 1997
1997.37

FIGURE. 37
Charlotte Wilson Hammond
(b. 1941)
Diamond Field, 1980
Oil on canvas, 144.5 x 182.2 cm
Purchased with funds provided by MT&T, Halifax, Nova Scotia, 1982
1982.3

FIGURE. 38
John Nesbitt
(b. 1928)
Joetoebloo, 1982
Epoxy-painted aluminum, 274.4 x 167.5 x 120.0 cm
Purchased with the assistance of the Canada Council Art Bank
Special Purchase Assistance Program, Ottawa, Ontario, 1983
1983.16

FIGURE. 39
Ruth Salter Wainwright
(1902 - 1984)
Cape Ray, Newfoundland, 1984
Pastel on paper, 41.0 x 50.8 cm
Gift of Isabel Wainwright, Halifax and
Harold Wainwright, Bridgewater, Nova Scotia, 2002
2002.57

FIGURE. 40
Carol Hoorn Fraser
(1930 - 1991)
The Equilibrists, 1977-1985
Oil on linen, 129.0 x 103.5 cm
Gift of John Fraser, Halifax, Nova Scotia, 2001
2001.22

FIGURE. 41
Alex Livingston
(b. 1958)
Haven, 1985
Oil on canvas, 226.6 x 238.7 cm
Purchased with funds provided by MT&T, Halifax, Nova Scotia, 1985
1985.44

FIGURE. 42
Nancy Edell
(b. 1942)
Waiting, 1986
Wool, acrylic and polyester fabrics on linen, 92.0 x 121.0 cm
Purchase, 1987
1987.4

FIGURE. 43
Joe Fafard
(b. 1942)
John Diefenbaker, 1986
Polychrome bronze, 9/12, 108.0 x 37.0 x 18.0 cm
Gift of Alex Colville, Wolfville, Nova Scotia, 1990
1990.7

FIGURE. 44
John Greer
(b. 1944)
Temple of the Order of Chaos, 1986
Italian marble, 68.9 x 109.2 x 25.4 cm
Purchased with funds raised by the Volunteer Committee
through ArtLottery '89 and '91, 1991
1991.19

FIGURE. 45
Christopher Pratt
(b. 1935)
Big Boat, 1986
Oil on canvas, 125.0 x 293.0 cm
Purchase supported by the Art Sales and Rental Society,
Halifax, Nova Scotia, 1987
1987.26

FIGURE. 46
Tom Forrestall
(b. 1936)
Island in the Ice, 1987
Egg tempera on masonite, 72.5 x 214.5 cm
Acquisition made possible with funds provided by
Christopher Ondaatje, Toronto, Ontario, 1994
1994.19

FIGURE. 47
Nyna Cropas
(b. 1949)
Kristallnacht, 1988
Acrylic on canvas, 182.5 x 366.0 cm
Purchased with the assistance of the Canada Council Art Bank
Special Purchase Assistance Program, Ottawa, Ontario, 1989
1989.31

FIGURE. 48
Ivan Eyre
(b. 1935)
Mountain Meadow, 1989
Acrylic on canvas, 142.0 x 304.8 cm
Gift of Sobey's Inc, Stellarton, Nova Scotia, 2001
2001.91

FIGURE. 49
Gerard Collins
(b. 1957)
Still-Life with Dying Tulips and Wallpaper Panelling, 1990
Oil on canvas, 152.2 x 136.8 cm
Purchase, 1990
1990.35

FIGURE. 50
Gerald Ferguson
(b. 1937)
Fish and Door, 1992
Enamel on canvas, painted wood, 213.3 x 223.5 cm
Purchased with funds provided by
Trimark Investment Management Inc., Toronto, Ontario, 1994
1994.38

FIGURE. 51
Gary Wilson
(b. 1951)
Tar Pond, Sydney, Cape Breton Co., N.S., July 1994
Silver gelatin print, 40.7 x 50.7 cm
Gift of the Artist, Halifax, Nova Scotia, 1999
1999.108

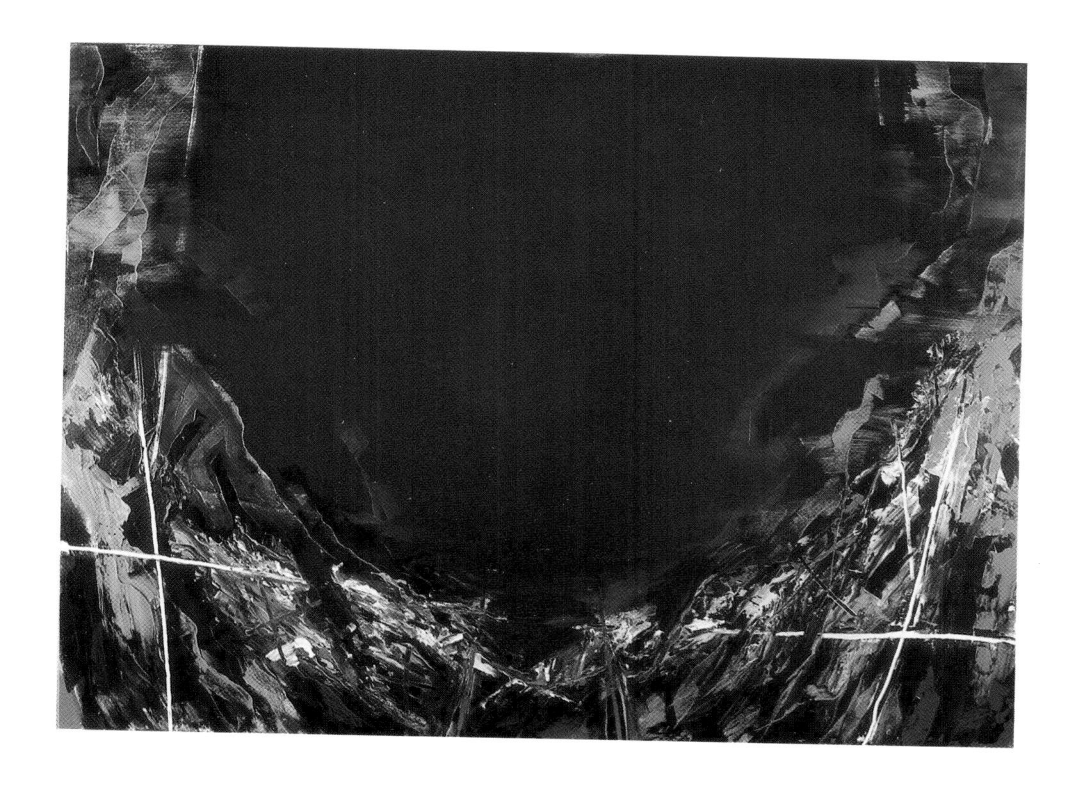

FIGURE. 52
Wayne Boucher
(b. 1943)
Blue, 1995
Acrylic on canvas, 134.7.0 x 183.0 cm
Gift of the Artist, Annapolis Royal, Nova Scotia, 2002
2002.7

FIGURE. 53
Mary Pratt
(b. 1935)
Sunday Dinner, 1996
Oil on canvas, 91.5 x 122.0 cm
Gift of the Artist, St. John's, Newfoundland, 1997
1997.82

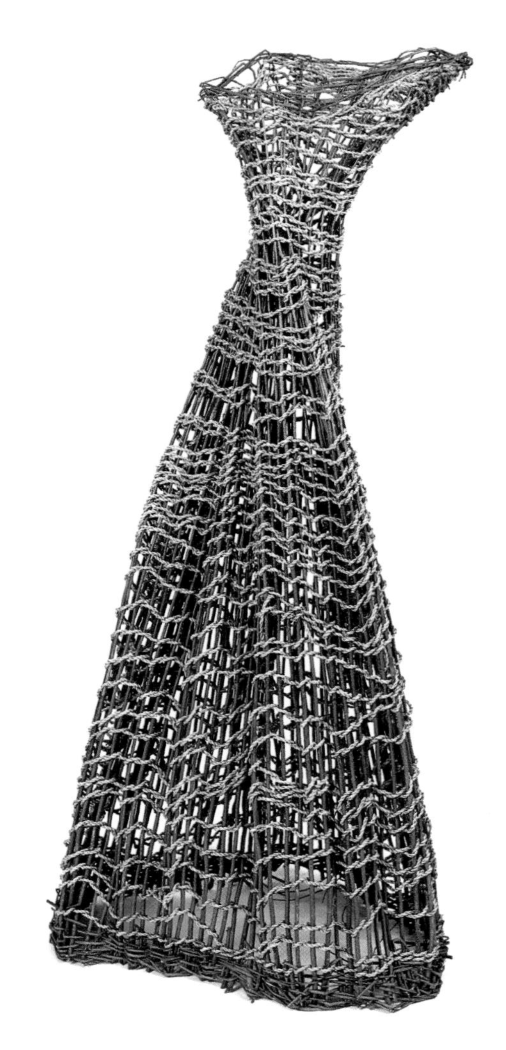

FIGURE. 54
Dawn MacNutt
(b. 1938)
Timeless Form #V, 1996-1997
Twined willow and seagrass, 170.0 x 66.0 cm
Gift of the Artist, Dartmouth, Nova Scotia,
in memory of Marian deWitt, 1997
1997.79

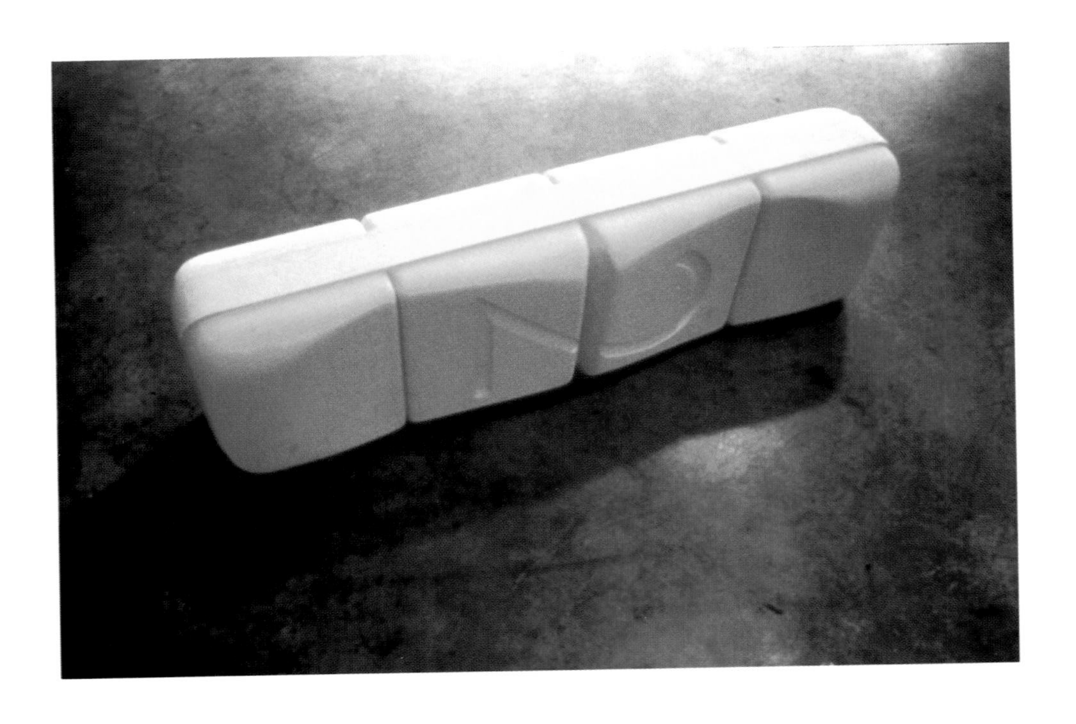

FIGURE. 55
Colleen Wolstenholme
(b. 1963)
Xanax 2mg, 1997
Carved plaster, 25.0 x 31.0 x 97.0 cm
Purchased with funds provided by The Canada Council for the Arts
Acquisition Assistance Programme and the Art Sales and Rental Society, 2001
2001.130

FIGURE. 56
Greg Forrest
(b. 1965)
Algoma, 1998
Painted steel and mixed media, 183.0 x 183.0 x 92.0 cm
Purchased with funds provided by The Canada Council for the Arts
Acquisition Assistance Programme and the Art Sales and Rental Society, 2001
2001.132

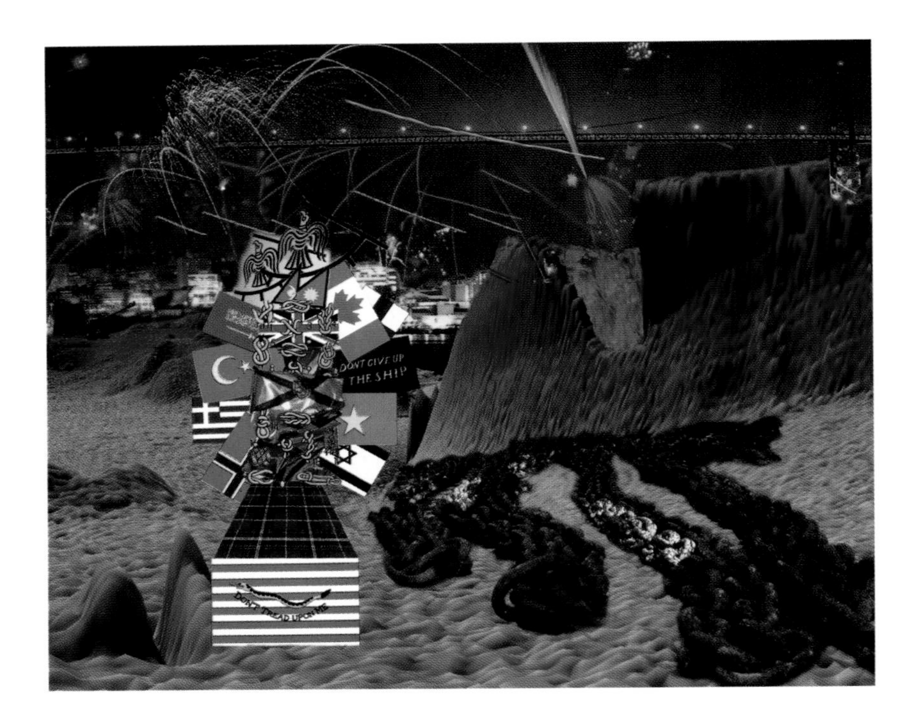

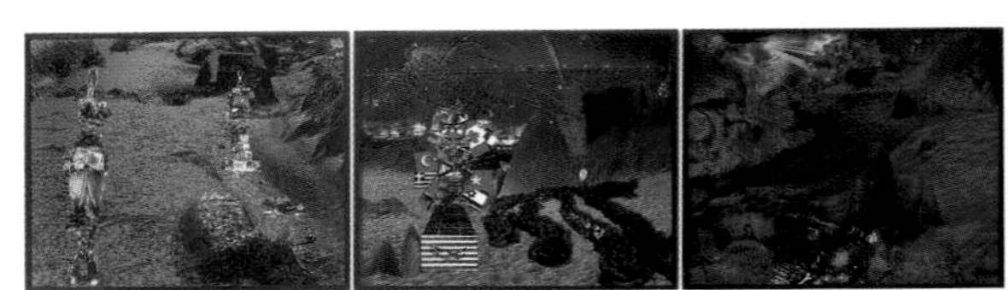

FIGURE. 57
David Askevold
(b. 1940)
Harbour Ghosts, Halifax, 1999
Ink jet print on coated paper, three panels, 122.0 x 151.8 cm each
Purchased with funds provided by The Canada Council for the Arts Acquisition Assistance Program and the AGNS Gallery Shop, 1999
1999.200

FIGURE. 58
Monica Tap
(b. 1962)
Untitled, 1999
Oil on canvas, 208.5 x 208.5 cm
Purchased with funds provided by The Canada Council for the Arts
Acquisition Assistance Programme and the AGNS Gallery Shop, 1999
1999.197

FIGURE. 59
Rebecca Fisk
(b. 1969)
Confessions of an Invisible Sister, 2001
Mixed media on canvas, 12 panels, 35.5 x 28.2 cm each
Purchased with funds provided by The Canada Council for the Arts
Acquisition Assistance Programme and Private Donors, 2001
2001.121

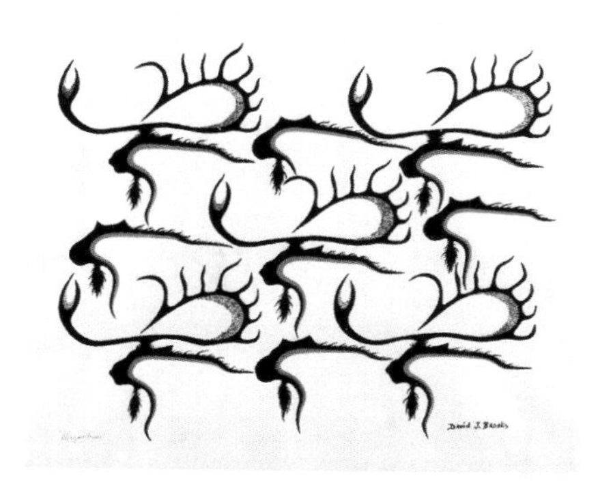

FIRST NATIONS AND INUIT ART

FIRST NATIONS AND INUIT ART

With art there is voice.

The Art Gallery of Nova Scotia's holdings of First Nations and Inuit art evidence changes in attitude, knowledge, and understanding, as society-at-large comes to terms with an art force that existed before European contact, and continues, revitalized and replenished by those artists who now create new and vibrant work.

First Nations and Inuit art are divided into separate categories at the AGNS. Inuit art has its own history, and Inuit culture is quite distinct from that of the First Nations, which in itself is quite diverse. As well, sophisticated marketing of Inuit art has made it attractive to mainstream collectors, uniquely so. With the possible exception of West Coast First Nations art, this has not been the case where most First Nations art is concerned.

The development of a First Nations and Inuit collection at the AGNS entails recognition of the political relationship that exists between each people, and with the federal government. Inuit art blossomed under interested guidance and became a cottage industry from the late 1950s, and the significant source of income for many communities in the far north, thanks to marketing schemes and federal support. Doors were opened to markets and major galleries in the United States, Europe, and Asia.

With much less support, Haida, Salish, and other West Coast artists have also received attention, with marketing based solely on the traditional or primitive look. In the North, the Inuit quickly became aware that the work being purchased by local southern-run art co-ops could not reference the contemporary. Depictions of airplanes, snowmobiles, or wooden homes caused alarm and were deemed unacceptable. The introduction of printmaking was originally frowned upon by these co-ops, and the production of colour prints also raised concern. In the early 1970s, the Inuit began to assume control of the co-ops and allow contemporary work to be marketed. On the West Coast, the anthropological viewpoint has only recently been discarded as the standard of authenticity and value.

The Art Gallery of Nova Scotia has a substantial collection of Inuit art, with seventy-seven pieces acquired since 1980, when Arnold and Kate Hoffman donated the Osuitok Ipeelee print, *Weasel*. The collection also includes thirty-three pieces of First Nations art, which began with the 1979 purchase of *Totem Pole* (artist unknown). *Totem Pole* is an example of what was expected of Aboriginal artists then, even though such artists as Alex Janvier, Bob Boyer, and Robert Houle were already working in a non-traditional or contemporary style.

In Atlantic Canada, Shirley Bear, Philip Young, and Alan Syliboy were in the early stages of their artistic careers.

Over the past twenty years, attitudes toward First Nations contemporary art and its parameters have changed. Recent acquisitions, such as Charles Doucette's *Untitled (Flag)* sculptures and Jane Ash Poitras' *Pink Shamans* (Fig. 68) exemplify this change. Masterworks of Aboriginal art have always existed, as every Nation has had its masters, but for too long those who governed public collections knew little about them. Anthropologists were the authorities on Aboriginal art, but their training and academic approach would only permit categorization of these items as artefacts. Contemporary First Nations artists in Canada have long voiced their concerns, and today their struggle is paying off. Today's First Nations artists now draw on their own creative history and produce meaningful works that define their place within global parameters.

In 1984, the AGNS acquired two significant First Nations works. Allen Angeconeb's *Four Profiles of Mother Earth* (Fig. 64) is a seemingly simplistic etching that is almost minimalist in appearance. One may not, at first, recognize the Eastern Woodland style of the Ojibway and Algonquin peoples influencing its creation, but upon close examination, Angeconeb's profiles seem to be similar in style, if not more authentically precise. It is a good example of this artist's early art-making, and one of the small treasures of this collection. Also collected that year was *Embryo* by Norval Morrisseau (Fig. 61), known as the father of the Eastern Woodland style of painting. Although not a prime example from this artist's repertoire of masterworks, it does demonstrate the liberal brushstrokes on a painted background with which Morrisseau experimented during the early to mid-1970s.

From 1980 to 1990, the AGNS collected twenty-three Inuit works, including such masterworks as Kenojuak Ashevak's *Sentinel Owl* (Fig. 60), Jessie Oonark's *Big Woman*, and Osuiuk Ipeelee's graceful stone carving, *Sedna, Mother of the Sea Beasts* (Fig. 63), a gift from Alma Houston in early 1984. Ashevak's *Sentinel Owl* is part of a series of several bird images created in the 1970s, and similar in its interpretation to that of her more famous *Enchanted Owl*. *Sentinel Owl* is as colourful as it is intriguing, the extended feathers and the saucer eyes creating an authoritative gaze that also suggests a strong spiritual quality.

Migration by David Brooks (Fig. 65), acquired in 1990, was actually the first piece of art by a Mi'kmaq artist collected by the AGNS. Brooks received much of his training from fellow Mi'kmaq artist Phillip Young. Influenced by the popular Eastern Woodland style, *Migration*, with it's liquid lines and flowing design, is reminiscent of the work of another principal Eastern Woodland-style painter, Benjamin Chee Chee. Brooks continued to work with and master this style of painting before coming into his own. His most recent art features symbols of his own Mi'kmaq nationality, and he is beginning to express a more personal approach to social and political concerns, often referring to place and identity rather than legend and aesthetics. Lance Belanger's *Untitled* (Fig. 66) was one of the major purchases made from the 1993 AGNS exhibition, *Pe'l A'tukwey*. Roger Simon's exquisite *Woman With A Gun* (Fig. 67) was also purchased out of this exhibition, although not until 1995.

Lance Belanger is a well-rounded artist with a modernist approach, one of the new generation of reconstructionist artists, who cleverly uses European paraphernalia to express contemporary First Nations grievances, regarding a vast range of issues. In this piece of slick, black enamel we can see the integration of computer circuit boards and a braid of sweetgrass arranged to form a butterfly, the metamorphic life of which symbolizes the balance between the spiritual and physical worlds of the Maliseet of New Brunswick. Belanger intrigues the viewer with yet another layer of meaning, involving the intercourse between technology and tradition. By using circuit boards and sweetgrass, Belanger opens up a narrative and discourse addressing the present human experience. Like a wise shaman, he leaves us to our own conclusions.

In 1994, Charles Fowler gifted the AGNS with a collection of sixteen pieces of Inuit art by such highly acclaimed artists as Abraham Anghik, Kiakshuk, and Sheouak. Anghik's *Lumiuk and the Whales* is typical of the work purchased by the southern-run co-ops of the 1960s. It is a strong graphic image depicting a pod of stylized whales passing two equally stylized hunters on the shoreline. It is mysterious and ancient looking, and powerfully rendered.

Margaret Johnson's *Untitled* (Fig. 62) is a wonderfully produced textile piece. Its earthy colours and applied patterns and beadwork evoke designs on the women's dresses the artist remembers from childhood. She skillfully uses an intimate knowledge of her culture to produce work that is deeply rooted in the Mi'kmaq tradition, while at the same time displaying a contemporary flare.

Alan Syliboy is one of Nova Scotia's most prominent artists. *Tuft's Cove Survivor* (Fig. 70) is one of his rare political pieces, and very prominent in the collection, as it gives an Aboriginal perspective to the devastating Halifax Explosion of 1917 that nearly destroyed the Tufts Cove Mi'kmaq community. Shortly after, the community was removed from the Dartmouth waterfront and relocated inland at Indianbrook Reserve and Cole Harbour Reserve. This was the Mi'kmaq's last access to Chebucto, the Big Harbour, a loss seldom noted but added to the hardships of this small, almost forgotten community.

Charles Doucette is one of Nova Scotia's most promising artists, and his postmodernist work often tackles the contemporary issues affecting his community. While utilizing a wide range of materials, he works primarily with sculpture, often incorporating found objects. *Signals: A Communiqué From Terra*

Nullis (Fig. 69) consists of several empty television screens that have been attached to a thick sheet of shaped plywood, with each screen relaying messages suggestive of specific technological failures: static with a woven diagonal pattern; a blank screen, which, upon closer examination, reveals etchings of a series of eight-pointed Mi'kmaq stars; and a screen showing garbage and debris covering a ceremonial stone pipe, a reflection on an era of simpler technology. The piece is shaped to outline the facial profile of the artist's son (with an antenna-like wire to form the eye), bridging the work, and all its implications, to the present generation. Doucette often challenges the acceptable perspective with which to view art. *Signals: A Communiqué from Terra Nullis* was meant to be set against the wall at floor level, making viewing uncomfortable, and suggestive of the inconvenience people experience when computers fail or a TV signal is interrupted.

There are fifteen First Nation artists and forty-three Inuit artists represented in the AGNS Permanent Collection. From Abraham Angik's traditional graphic imagery to Charles Doucette's postmodernist sculptures, the entire collection has made a difference as to how First Nations and Inuit art is perceived. Each artist has taken a step on the path toward a better understanding between Aboriginal and non-Aboriginal societies in Canada. Art remains a mystery, and a mysterious source of power. When we consider the artistic accomplishment represented here, we can feel the spirit of our ancestors and the magic of this land, the power of the creative impulse, and know the workings of imagination and determination. The future has never looked more promising for our artists to speak through their art: in the practice of their creativity, in drawing from their history, and in sharing that history with an enlightened, curious public.

Jim Logan
Former Associate Curator First Nations Art

NOTE
In the 1970s, the term "First Nations" was adopted by Status and Non-status Aboriginal (and in some cases Métis) people to replace the term "Indian" which was viewed as an offensive term. Inuit people have a different political relationship with the Government of Canada and are not covered by the Indian Act. Métis people, like the Inuit, are also not covered by the Indian Act. The Canadian Constitution Act of 1982 recognizes Aboriginal People as Indian, Inuit, and Métis. The Indian Act defines Indian "as a person pursuant to the Indian Act who is registered or entitled to be registered." This registration is commonly known as Status.

FIGURE. 60
Kenojuak Ashevak
(b. 1927)
Sentinel Owl, 1970
Stonecut and stencil on paper, 44/50, 59.7 x 82.5 cm
Purchase, 1982
1982.21

FIGURE. 61
Norval Morrisseau
(B. 1932)
Embryo, c. 1975
Acrylic on board; 106.5 x 61.0 cm
Gift of John deWitt, Halifax, Nova Scotia, 1984
1984.200

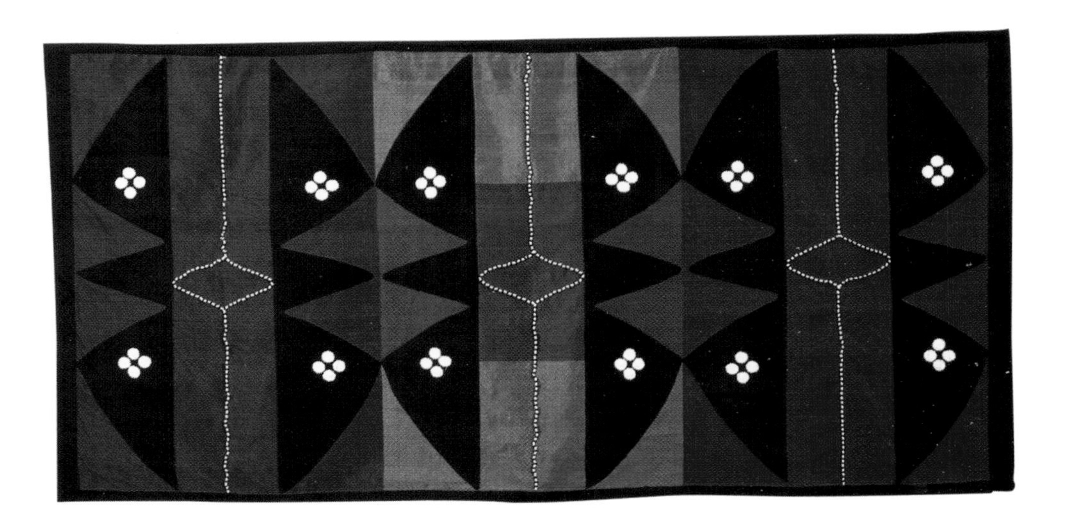

FIGURE. 62
Margaret Johnson
(b. 1915)
Untitled, 1979
Silk, beads and cotton, 86.5 x 175.0 cm
Gift of Dianne O'Neill, Halifax, Nova Scotia, 1998
1998.12

FIGURE. 63
Osuitok Ipeelee
(b. 1923)
Sedna, Mother of the Sea Beasts, 1981
Carved serpentine stone, 56.5 x 29.5 x 14.5 cm
Gift of Alma Houston, LaHave, Nova Scotia, 1984
1984.1

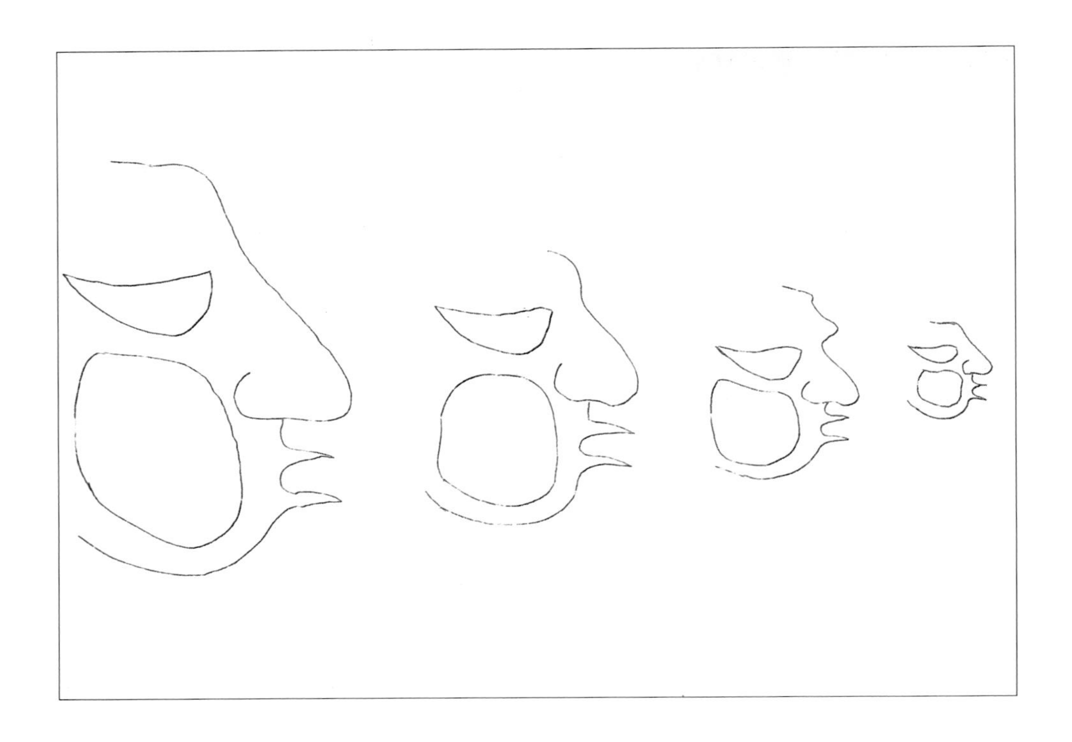

FIGURE. 64
Allen Angeconeb
(b. 1955)
Four Profiles of Mother Earth, 1984
Etching on paper, 14/16, 25.5 x 38.0 cm
Gift of Jim and Pat Lotz, Halifax, Nova Scotia,
in memory of the Hutcheons of Oldmeldrum, Aberdeenshire, 1984
1984.25

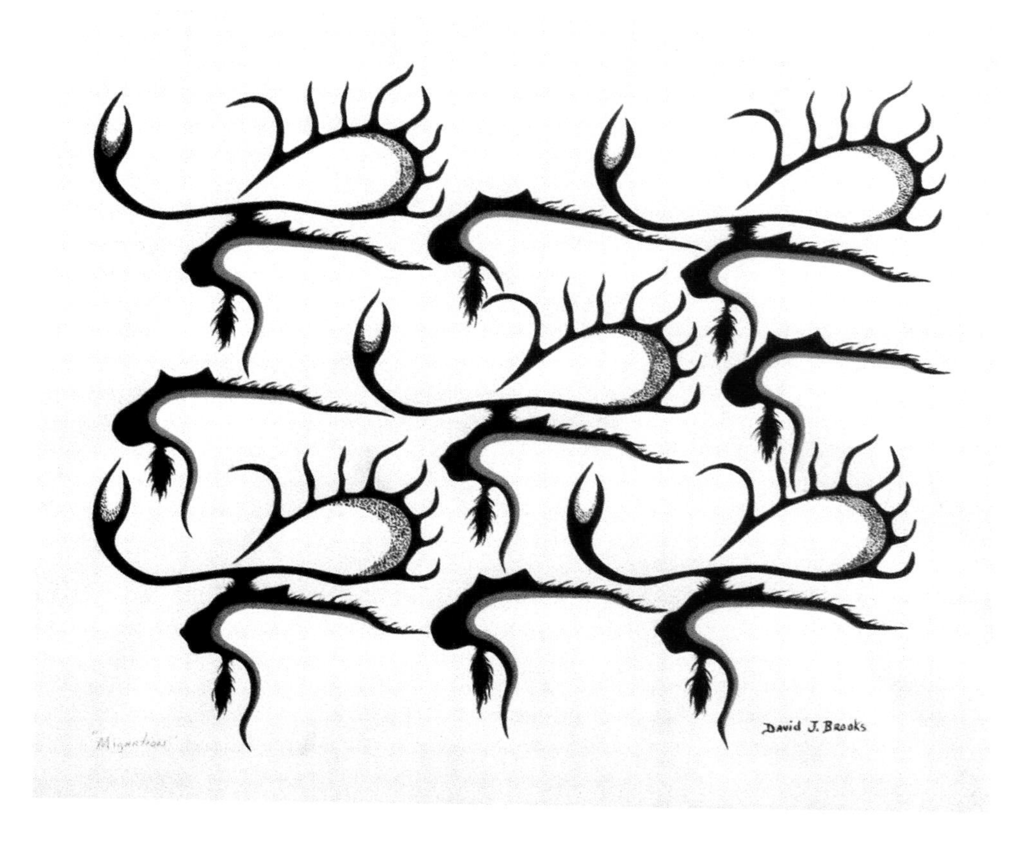

FIGURE. 65
David J. Brooks
(b. 1950)
Migration, 1990
Acrylic on paper, 48.0 x 56.0 cm
Gift of Statistics Canada, Halifax, Nova Scotia, 1990
1990.64

FIGURE. 66
Lance Belanger
(b. 1956)
Untitled, 1991
Enamel and mixed media on board, 91.5 x 183.0 cm
Purchased with funds provided by MT&T, Halifax, Nova Scotia, 1993
1993.126

FIGURE. 67
Roger Simon
(b. 1954)
Woman with a Gun, 1992
Oil on paper; 50.5 x 40.0 cm
Purchased with funds provided by
the Art Sales and Rental Society, Halifax, Nova Scotia, 1995
1995.2

FIGURE. 68
Jane Ash Poitras
(b. 1951)
Pink Shamans, 1996
Mixed media on canvas, 244.0 x 186.7 cm
Purchased with the support of the Canada Council
Acquisition Assistance Program and
the Art Sales and Rental Society, Halifax, Nova Scotia, 1997
1997.130

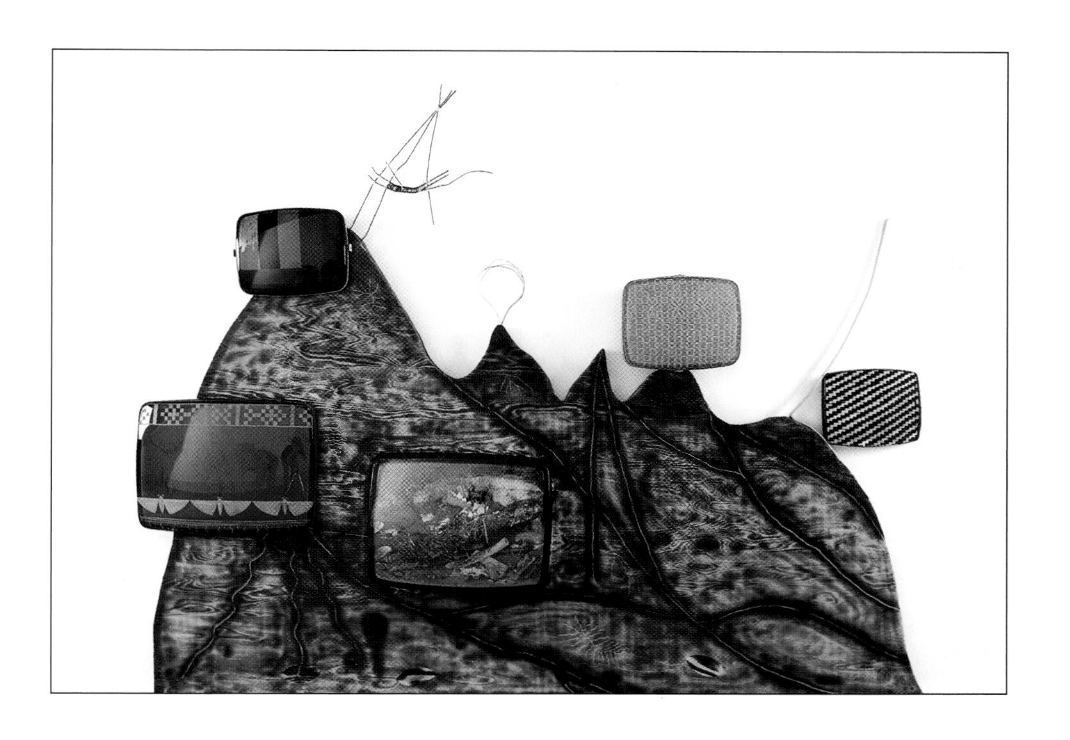

FIGURE. 69
Charles Doucette
(b. 1962)
Signals: A Communiqué From Terra Nullis, 1999
Television screens, found materials on plywood, 152.0 x 188.0 x 10.0 cm
Purchased with funds provided by the Canada Council for the Arts
Acquisition Assistance Program and the AGNS Gallery Shop, 1999
1999.198

FIGURE. 70
Alan Syliboy
(b. 1952)
Tuft's Cove Survivor, 1999
Acrylic, watercolour pencil, ink, and photo transfer
on illustration board, 76.0 x 101.5 cm
Purchased with funds provided by the Canada Council for the Arts
Acquisition Assistance Program and the AGNS Gallery Shop, 1999
1999.202

FOLK ART

FOLK ART

The Art Gallery of Nova Scotia's Folk Art collection of more than 500 works began in 1976 when the *Folk Art of Nova Scotia* exhibition was organized at our Coburg Road location, then toured nationally. The inspiration was Russell Harper's book and exhibition, *People's Art: Naive Art in Canada*. The idea was to showcase a sampling of the best of folk art, from the earliest times to the early 1970s. After a period of research, it was determined that much of the nineteenth-century material was unavailable, and that the most significant early works had been included in Dr. Harper's exhibition at the National Gallery of Canada. However, Nova Scotia had a wealth of living folk artists creating innovative and dynamic work, so it was decided to feature provincial selections from the twentieth century only. A special committee of folk-art collectors and curators was convened. Chris Huntington, Ellen Huntington, Gerald Ferguson, Murray Stewart, and Bruce Ferguson worked with me and with researchers Graham Metson, Nelda Swinton, and writers Dr. Helen Creighton and Dr. Marie Elwood.

The folk art featured in this seminal exhibition spanned seventy years, most of it executed between 1965 and 1975 by artists who were still active. Represented were many different styles, techniques, and mediums conveying the dynamic spirit and inventiveness of people whose creations constitute a special contribution to the cultural development and visual heritage of Nova Scotia.

In 1976, one of the best-known folk artists was Collins Eisenhauer from Scarsdale, Lunenburg County, who began carving at the age of 66 and came to be recognized as a pioneer in inspiring the appreciation of folk art as artistic expression in Nova Scotia. Although he had no time for his art during his working life, he recalled his boyhood pleasure at making drawings and small paintings. Collins, a labourer throughout his life, worked for many years as a logger in the Belliveau Woods. His wooden sculptures, now internationally appreciated, range from the miniature to the monumental, from the erotic to the religious. Among his best-known works is his *Self-portrait,* 1976 (Fig. 83), depicting the artist carving a decoy.

Another of the great carvers included in the exhibition, and represented here by the sculpture of a *Fisherman,* c.1970 (Fig. 78), is Ralph Boutilier, born at Boutilier's Point. From 1936, Ralph often painted in his spare time, selling his paintings and taking local commissions. A multi-talented individual, having been a barber, an electrician, a carpenter, a boat builder, a sign painter, and a fisherman, he took up carving again at the age of 70.

The work of Cape Breton carver Sidney Howard appeared in the original *Folk Art of Nova Scotia* exhibition, and in our *Nova Scotia Collects* series, with *The Philip Brooks Collection: Sidney Howard's Beacons and Strays.* Sidney was a genuine people person. He carved numerous cats, fish, and a collection of birds. His larger works include *The Giant MacAskill*, and such Canadian celebrities as *Rita MacNeil, Stompin' Tom Connors*, and *John Diefenbaker*. Sidney carved pieces characterized by personal expression and personal discovery rather than by imitation or tradition. He left his pieces with a characteristic rawness in an effort to make them, if not a perfect likeness, then a product of the artist's personality. When Sidney moved to Albert Bridge, Cape Breton, in the 1960s, he created life-size figures and placed them in front of his house at the highway. As these beacons were sold, or stolen, others replaced them: politicians, fisherman, and Mounties, such as the AGNS *Mountie,* c.1981 (Fig. 84). In 2000, Dr. Philip Brooks generously donated to the Gallery a selection of folk art that included a strong representation of works by Sidney Howard.

Folk artist Joe Sleep, born at sea between England and Saint John, New Brunswick, was a jack-of-all-trades who took his creative ideas from magazines and newspapers, but also painted from his memories of life as a fisherman and as a carnival worker with the Bill Lynch Shows. Joe was featured in an AGNS exhibition curated by Bruce Ferguson, then Director/Curator at Dalhousie Art Gallery. Joe began painting after receiving encouragement from nurses at the Halifax Infirmary, where he was a patient in 1973. While his cat became his trademark image, and a best seller, one of the most interesting works in the AGNS collection is *Ship and Creatures* (Fig. 82), a lithograph on paper completed when he was given a place to work and his first show at the Nova Scotia College of Art and Design. Following Joe Sleep's death, the AGNS was the recipient of a collection of works from his estate.

Albert Lohnes was a sailor in Ragged Harbour, Lunenburg County. Once, noting that his captain had a problem—he was sliding all over his chair while at sea—Lohnes' solution was to crochet some red, white and blue yarn around the chair. While the captain would still roll back and forth with the sea, he could not slip off. Albert began to knit chairs seriously around 1970, and his total output never exceeded twenty, of which the slightly earlier *White and Blue Crocheted Rocking Chair,* c.1965 (Fig. 77) is prime.

The Gallery has been fortunate to have the support of such folk-art collectors as Chris Huntington, who have given generously to enhance the collection. *A Life of Its Own,* an AGNS exhibition, with catalogue, curated by Ken Martin, acknowledges Chris Huntington's role in the resurgence of folk art here from 1975 to 1995. The history of the folk art of Nova Scotia had been highlighted earlier in the AGNS exhibition, *Spirit of Nova Scotia: Traditional Decorative Folk Art 1780-1930,* with guest curator Richard Field; it toured Canada to rave reviews. The works shown continue to speak for themselves, each an individual statement offering spontaneity, simplicity, and in many cases, humour.

The folk artist finds the direct solution to technical or aesthetic problems, displaying his or her integrity and honesty of purpose, and the resourceful use of available materials. The vitality and freshness of this approach gives folk art a universal appeal. Applying colour and form in an intuitive and simplistic manner is part of the appeal of folk art—an expression of inherent joy.

Maud Lewis is a legendary figure. *The Illuminated Life of Maud Lewis* which, beginning in 1997, toured nationally, was part of a grander AGNS project celebrating this prolific Marshalltown artist. This included a book and a CD on the artist and her work, the development of products using her imagery, a memorial on the original Lewis property in Marshalltown, and the dedication of an AGNS exhibition space, the Scotiabank Maud Lewis Gallery (Fig. 76). The painted house is Maud's largest work of art, with almost every surface of the tiny 4.1 x 3.8 m. structure decorated with her delightful images—windows, stairs, even the stove. After Maud's death in 1970 and husband Everett's in 1979, the Maud Lewis Painted House Society of Digby took steps to protect the structure, but the building continued to deteriorate. In 1984, the Province purchased the little house for the AGNS. The restoration process, under the capable supervision of fine art conservator Laurie Hamilton, was completed in 1998, and the AGNS display was opened to the public in June of that year.

Folk sculpture in Nova Scotia grew out of utilitarian needs and the individual situations in which early settlers found themselves in a new land. The diversity of immigrant patterns here has added to the richness of our folk art. By 1850, as Nova Scotian society began to take shape, prosperity brought with it a cultural resurgence and a Nova Scotian spirit. A fine example of folk art from this early period is James Hertle's *Black Figure in a Dancing Position,* c.1865 (Fig. 71). Hertle was a ship's carver at Dartmouth's Williams' Shipyard. Its black, yellow, and red polychrome paint is original, and the position of the hands and feet indicate that the figure is beginning to perform a dance. One of the finest nineteenth-century carvings anywhere, it is a national treasure.

Another side to folk-art expression is represented in the 1981 AGNS exhibition, *Gameboards*, curated by Richard Field. Post-exhibition, the Bird/Kobyashi collection of gameboards was acquired with the financial support of the Canadian Cultural Property Import and Export Review Board. *The Mason Family Parcheesi Gameboard* (Fig. 73) is an outstanding example of Lunenburg County decorative art, the colour scheme and the five-point star motif common to the region. The painted house in the centre, which acts as "home" for the Parcheesi board, is an appropriate and a delightful touch. Gameboards are important sociocultural artefacts and reflect the behavioural patterns of both the maker and the user.

With the establishment, in 1988, of a permanent home for the Art Gallery of Nova Scotia in a prominent downtown location, a special folk art gallery was named in honour of benefactors Jack and Joan Craig.

Lower Prospect's Joe Norris found himself in the same position as many of the other folk artists who developed an illness and took up their art as a second career. In 1973, at the age of 49, Joe, unable to continue as a fisherman after a heart attack, became a painter, producing brightly coloured pictures of the world around him, with no preconceived ideas, no drawing or sketching experience. His works depict Nova Scotia's landscapes and seascapes, as on the 1975 *Painted Chest* (Fig. 81). In 2000, the nationally touring *Joe Norris: Painted Visions of Nova Scotia* celebrated the extraordinary work of a very ordinary person, his art representing the "peaceable kingdom" of Nova Scotia.

A self-made man of many talents, Charles Macdonald made an important contribution to the political, social, economic, and artistic life of his community and province. His own life exemplified the boundless energy and ambition, as well as the spirit, of Canada's "common man." A 1980 AGNS exhibition curated by Patrick Condon Laurette chronicled Macdonald's life and artistic accomplishments, of which *Steam Mill* (Fig. 72) is a first-rate example of both painting and frame carving. He was a master with the medium of concrete, creating and decorating his concrete house in Centreville and concrete cottages in Huntington Point. The Charles Macdonald House of Centreville Society has preserved the house, cottages, and an art collection, as a public art museum celebrating this uncommon common man.

Evelyn Dickie was born in Meaghers Grant in 1903, and later lived in Massachusetts and New Hampshire. Her traditional quilts are derived from a vivid imagination, as is the *Map of Meaghers Grant* (Fig. 80) depicting her native village.

The new generation of folk artists includes Leo Naugler, born in 1956. He worked on provincial roads for the Department of Highways, and later as a woodsman, a general fix-it man, and as an autobody repairman, whence come some of the interesting textural features in his work. He began painting and carving in 1989, and his work is ambitious, imaginative, and prolific. Leo's work was included in the *Nova Scotia Folk Art: Canada's Cultural Heritage* international traveling exhibition. *Royal Goose Fountain,* 1994 (Fig. 86) is part of a large gift made by astute collector Iris E. Newman, who has been a special friend of the AGNS.

Lorne Reid (see Fig. 85) was born in Dominion, Cape Breton. He aspired to be an artist from a fairly early age, but took to the road for sixteen years, with a short stint in the Navy along the way. At the age of 33, Lorne returned to Cape Breton to give his art a serious shot. During 1987-1988, a folk-art style took hold. Lorne's paintings and painted sculptures are imaginative and often complex. There are two sides to his work: a light, carefree, and happy approach; and a much deeper, more contemplative vision. His is some of the most original art to come out of Nova Scotia. Lorne was also instrumental in discovering and encouraging other well-known Cape Breton folk artists.

Hooked rugs have been made in Nova Scotia since the second quarter of the nineteenth century. Unadorned rugs would have kept floors equally warm, but most rug-makers were inspired to add their personal designs and colours, resulting in bold and dynamic works of art. While geometric and floral patterns were most common, some makers deviated from the norm and introduced drawn shapes and freer, more imaginative design. *Hooked Rug (With our Hands/Clasped...)*, c.1940 (Fig. 75) by an unknown artist is a powerful expression of Commonwealth solidarity in the early days of World War II.

Peter Frotten's *Queen of Seas* ship's model, c.1930 (Fig. 74) is a singular piece within the active tradition of ship carving prevalent in Nova Scotia over two centuries. Such a fine example, together with a decorated base, is especially rare. It was carved near Lockport, Nova Scotia.

Walter Cook (Fig. 79) was born in Sherbrook, Nova Scotia, and spent twenty-three years in the army, traveling widely. He took up carving at the age of 10, and following his retirement from the Canadian Armed Forces, resumed his hobby. He had about given it up again by 1978, when Chris Huntington met and encouraged him. Walter Cook became a mainstay of the Nova Scotia Folk Art Festival.

The AGNS Permanent Collection contains and presents the folk art of Nova Scotia, an integral part of Canada's cultural heritage. The works demonstrate the spirit of Nova Scotia's culturally diverse people, who have expressed themselves in equally diverse forms. The importance of these works derives from their status as individual art objects, and also from their historical and cultural associations.

When we observe the production of the current generation of folk artists, we can conclude that our smaller population, less influenced by industrialization and post-industrialization, has been able to preserve a folk tradition lost elsewhere. Our folk art descends from a shared past, but our social conditions have permitted its continuous development. Within this tradition, self-expression and imagination are vital. Awareness of both the folk community and the outside, now largely urban, world influences the folk artist, who draws on both for inspiration. The concerns of the avant-garde art world hold no appeal for folk artists.

Art created by the ordinary person is one of the healthiest of visual expressions. The AGNS folk art collection clearly demonstrates that the creative approach making it possible is a spontaneous phenomenon that exists to please the viewer. Here is an art form that has emerged out of the heart and soul of our country, Nova Scotia in particular, as a tangible extension of the lives and experiences of its creators.

Bernard Riordon, O.C.
Director, and Curator Folk Art, 1973-2002

FIGURE. 71
James Hertle
(1842 - 1877)
Black Figure in a Dancing Position, c.1865
Polychrome wood, 126.0 x 34.5 x 32.5 cm
Acquisition made possible with the assistance of a grant approved by the Minister of Canadian Heritage, under the terms of the Cultural Property Export and Import Act and the Volunteer Special Events Committee through Art Lottery '94, sponsored by Nova Scotia Power Inc., 1993 and The Ondaatje Foundation, 1998
1993.181

FIGURE. 72
Charles Macdonald
(b. 1874 - 1967)
Steam Mill, Homestead Road, n.d.
Oil on canvas board, 55.8 x 76.0 cm
Purchased with funds provided by
The Craig Foundation, Halifax, Nova Scotia, 2002
2002.10

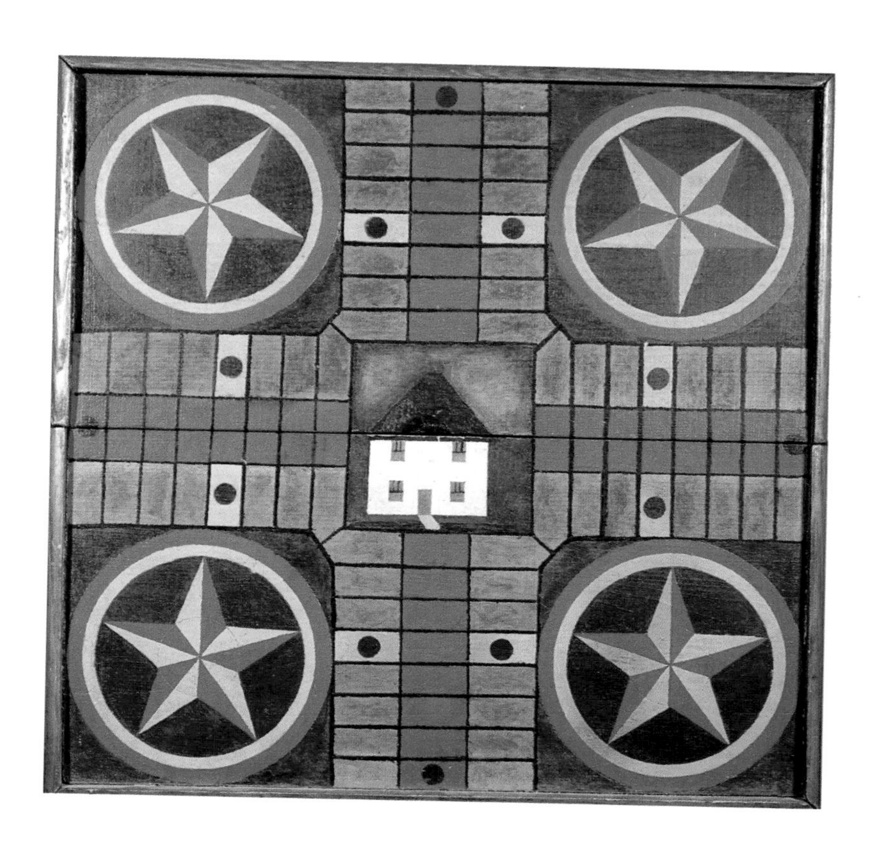

FIGURE. 73
Unknown
(20th century)
Mason Family Parcheesi Gameboard, c.1925
Polychrome wood, 54.8 x 55.3 cm
Purchased with funds from the Government of Canada, Ottawa under the terms of the Cultural Property Export and Import Act, 1992
1992.59

FIGURE. 74
Peter Frotten
(20th century)
Queen of Seas Model of Ship with Stand, c.1930
Polychrome wood, string and oil paint, 140.0 x 120.0 x 38.0 cm
Purchase, 1976
1976.35

FIGURE. 75
Unknown
(20th century)
Hooked Rug (With Our Hands / Clasped Jean Across / the Sea of Love), c.1940
Wool on burlap, homespun, 177.0 x 131.6 cm
Purchase, 1977
1977.29

FIGURE. 76
Maud Lewis House as installed
in the Scotiabank Maud Lewis Gallery

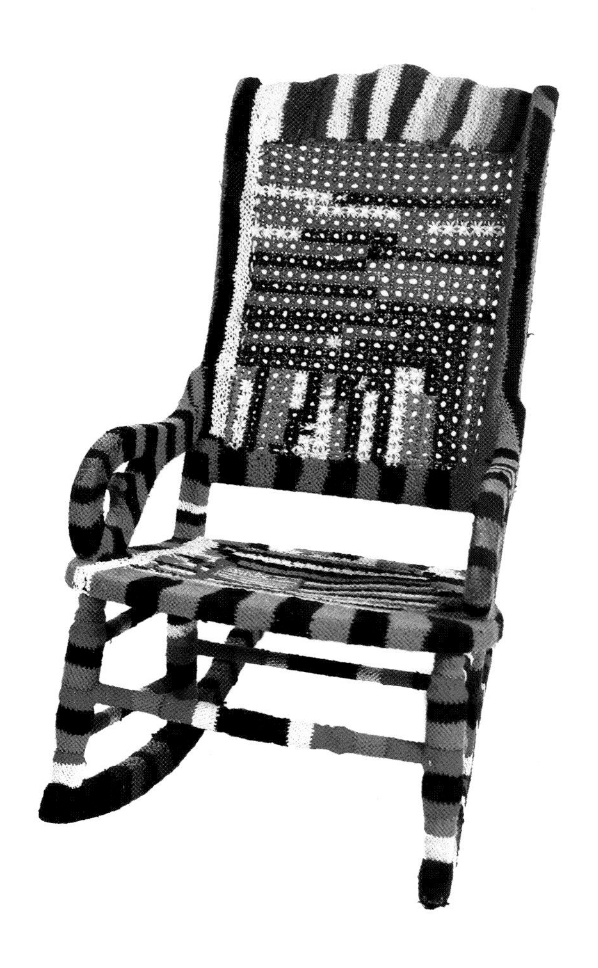

FIGURE. 77
Albert Lohnes
(1894 - 1977)
The Red, White and Blue Crocheted Rocking Chair, c.1965
Wool and wood, 88.0 x 33.0 x 31.0 cm
Gift of Chris Huntington, Mahone Bay, Nova Scotia, 1993
1993.19

FIGURE. 78
Ralph Boutilier
(1906 - 1989)
Fisherman, c.1970
Polychrome wood, oil, 145.0 x 59.0 x 21.0 cm
Purchase, 1977
1977.7

FIGURE. 79
Walter Cook
(1923 - 1991)
Trudeau, c.1974
Polychrome wood, 200.0 x 51.0 x 44.5 cm
Gift of Chris Huntington, Mahone Bay, Nova Scotia, 1993
1993.7

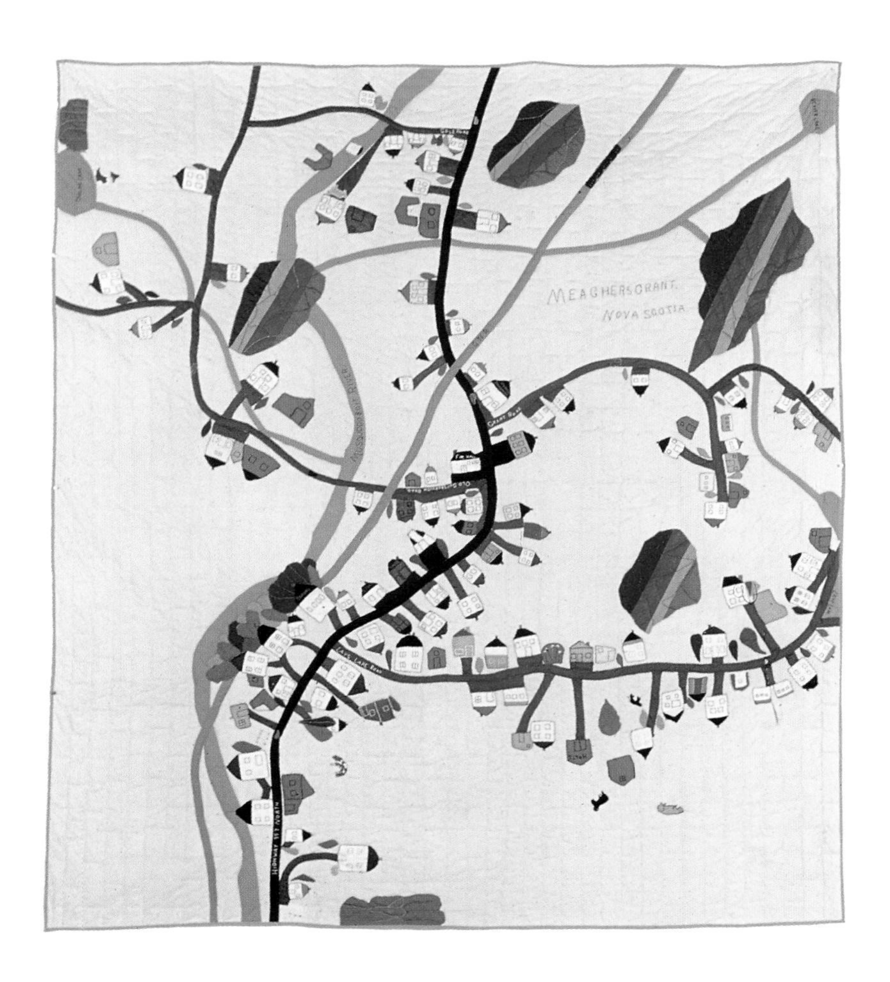

FIGURE. 80
Evelyn Dickie
(1903-1993)
Map of Meaghers Grant, 1975
Cotton, 222.5 x 197.0 cm
Purchase, 1977
1977.9

FIGURE. 81
Joe Norris
(1924 - 1996)
Painted Chest, 1975
Polychrome wood, 37.0 x 91.5 x 44.2 cm
Purchase, 1977
1977.21

FIGURE. 82
Joseph Sleep
(1914 - 1978)
Ship and Creatures, c.1976
Lithograph on paper, 12/70, 61.0 x 91.2 cm
Purchase, 1981
1981.25

FIGURE. 83
Collins Eisenhauer
Self-portrait, 1976
(1898 - 1979)
Polychrome wood, rubber and hair, 118.0 x 41.0 x 84.0 cm
Purchase, 1977
1977.14

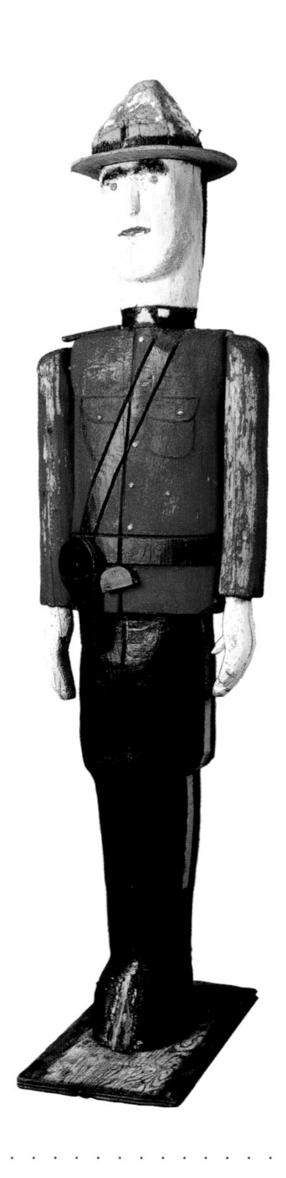

FIGURE. 84
Sidney Howard
(1913 - 1992)
Mountie, c.1981
Polychrome wood, plastic and steel, 187.0 x 48.5 x 61.0 cm
Gift of Dr. Philip J. Brooks, Sydney, Nova Scotia, 1999
1999.157

FIGURE. 85
Lorne Reid
(1954 - 1991)
Fishermen Bartering with Coalminers, 1987
Oil on masonite, 90.2 x 121.8 cm
Purchase, 1988
1988.18

FIGURE. 86
Leo Naugler
(b. 1956)
Royal Goose Fountain, 1994
Polychrome metal and wood, 178.0 x 147.0 x 120.0 cm
Gift of Iris E. Newman, Halifax, Nova Scotia, 1997, in honour of
Mark H. Newman, Shawna Newman Mirken and Amy F. P. Newman Brown
1997.245

CERAMICS

CERAMICS

In 1994, the Art Gallery of Nova Scotia opened the Lloyd and Jean Shaw Gallery. Jean Shaw had been a long-time supporter of the AGNS, and in addition to contributing the funds to establish a ceramics gallery, she loaned a number of works from her personal collection for the inaugural exhibition of contemporary studio ceramics. The AGNS is one of the very few public galleries to collect works in this major area of twentieth-century art. By preserving contemporary ceramic objects and recognizing their value as examples of powerful creative expression, the AGNS has bridged the long-perceived gap between folk and fine arts.

There are more than 150 works in this collection, including three works by recipients of the prestigious Saidye Bronfman Award, Canada's highest award for excellence in the crafts: Robin Hopper, Steven Heinemann, and Harlan House. The collection also includes the work of Walter Ostrom, a Jean Chalmers Award winner. Moreover, there are pieces by internationally renowned ceramists, including Wayne Higby, Andrea Gill, Alison Britton, Michael Casson, Brother Thomas, and Alan Caiger-Smith, as well as by two of the most famous British potters of the twentieth century, Bernard Leach and Lucie Rie.

Works by prominent local and Maritime potters are also included: Peter Powning, Tom Smith, Jane Donovan, Peter Bustin, Jim Smith, and Kathy Thompson. The mandate of the Art Gallery of Nova Scotia is to collect works by local, national, and international ceramists who have contributed to the community and have spent time in Nova Scotia. The collection has been developed with the purpose of educating and providing pleasure to the general public.

One of the highlights of the collection, *Untitled* (Fig. 95), is the work of Jean-Pierre Larocque, who is based in Montreal and has been a visiting lecturer at the Nova Scotia College of Art and Design. Larocque's depicted horses are glazed in layers, rather than painted, and are refired in the kiln many times. The construction process is largely intuitive. Working with two or three different batches of stoneware clay, which create different colours when fired, Larocque builds up layers and then strips them down, adding, subtracting, and amending until he finds the forms and proportions he likes. Over the course of creation, the acts of molding the works by hand, firing, glazing, and reshaping them again all fuse together into a single, jagged process. This balance between the work's fragmented appearance and its overall structural cohesion and aesthetic coherence may be its most striking feature.

Another significant piece is *Deruta's Geisha* (Fig. 96) by Andrea Gill, who has been a professor at the prestigious New York College of Ceramics at Alfred

University since 1984. Gill is mainly known for her large, winged vases in earthenware with majolica glazes (majolica is a term used to describe tin-glazed earthenware made in the Italian style). Her personal vision as an artist focuses on a format that is admittedly ancient. She is passionate about ceramic form as a site for personal expression. She has little interest in the old form-versus-function debate, choosing to make vases and bowls because such forms allow the most open interpretation of shape without losing the iconic identity of the object.

Deruta's Geisha, made in 2001, refers to the centre in Italy specifically known for its majolica, dating back to the fourteenth and fifteenth centuries. "Geisha" refers to the Japanese-influenced floral designs on the piece, the kimono wrapped around the figure, and to the Asian features of the face. Gill has lately been introducing female figurative elements into her winged vases, and this piece incorporates both the well-known wings and the figuration. The size of *Deruta's Geisha* gives her room to explore colour, shape, and pattern. Her devotion to surface patterning satisfies her love of the stylized image, and demonstrates her positive response to all things decorative. She feels that ceramics is the ideal medium in which to combine surface colour and three-dimensional form.

Wayne Higby, another teacher at Alfred University, demonstrates, in his tile piece, *Monument Beach* (Fig. 94), the powerful influence landscapes and landscape painting have had on him since his earliest years as an artist. Higby has discovered, in the ancient Japanese firing technique of raku, a way of controlling his colour as a painter would, using his glazes as though they were pigments on the edge of a painter's palette, and combining the process of reduction and oxidation in the same work. Higby plays with the two-dimensional/three-dimensional dichotomy. He breaks the 'picture' plane with an actual sculptural/architectural protrusion that depicts a landscape element which also acts as a support or brace to the painting/sculpture. The viewer's eye is drawn toward the meeting of water and sky at the horizon on the left of the tile, but at the same time is called to focus on the gap or negative space. The picture plane is disrupted, not only by this negative space and the three-dimensional protrusion of the rocks at the base, but also by the deep incisions surrounding the notch. *Monument Beach,* like most of Higby's work, is a fusion of East and West that delays and redirects the act of seeing art, architecture, nature, and illusion.

Blue Apron Pot (Fig. 91), another valuable work, made by the internationally recognized British ceramist, Alison Britton, is built out of slabs of clay, sprinkled with crumbs of dry clay to add texture. The piece is laid in with marks of slip (liquid clay), and colour, which eventually binds the form. Each side is different, yet the whole is dynamic. The surface of *Blue Apron Pot* is not a glazed skin but rather a piece of canvas. The painting presented is not repetitive, reinforcing Britton's goal to make each facet of her pots unique. Alison acknowledges that the human body is a central focus in her work, and here it is subtly integrated with holistic, oblique references to the physical self: lines, wrinkled skin, awkward limbs, protrusions, and nuances of feeling and thought.

Alice Egan Hagen, the "pioneer potter" of Mahone Bay, Nova Scotia, is represented by her hand-painted porcelain *Jug* (Fig. 87), a landscape painting in the round. Hagen also experimented in local clays and glaze materials, and gave regular summer classes in pottery. One of her last students, Homer Lord, began to teach at the Nova Scotia College of Art in 1949, remained there for thirty-eight years, and had a wide influence throughout the province. We are fortunate to have a number of works from his private collection, among them *Covered Jardinière* (Fig. 88), a functional earthenware piece with simple decoration and glazing.

The studio pottery movement in Nova Scotia, in effect founded by Alice Egan Hagen, continues today through the influence of the Nova Scotia College of Art and Design, with Walter Ostrom at its head. An inspired maker and teacher, Ostrom has had a tremendous effect on a whole generation of ceramists in Canada and the United States. In his *Fish Vase with Greek Pot* (Fig. 89), the ornament from an ancient Greek pot is the image on a fish vase, the double fish being a symbol of marital bliss. There is an ambiguity between what is real and what is not, a trick used by the Baroque mannerists. Ostrom unites archetypal images of West and East with what might be called serious humour.

Jug (Fig. 92), by the master British potter Michael Casson, is an excellent example of stoneware clay with a salt glaze. Salt glazing is achieved by throwing common salt into the kiln when the temperature is about 1,000°c, producing a hard glaze with a texture resembling the skin of an orange.

In *Large Globular Vase* (Fig. 90), Brother Thomas has perfected the fugitive technique of reducing the oxygen in the kiln firing to make the copper contained in the glaze covering the porcelain piece turn red. The vase is a masterpiece of wheel throwing and a fine illustration of the work that has led to the recognition of this former Nova Scotian ceramist as an iconic figure in the United States.

And in *Majestic Ridge* (Fig. 93), Alberta-born Les Manning laminates stoneware and porcelain to simulate the rock formations and glaciers of the Rocky Mountains, within which setting he headed up the ceramics department at the Banff Centre for twenty years.

The collection of contemporary studio ceramics assembled by the Art Gallery of Nova Scotia positions it in the forefront of Canadian public galleries.

Alexandra McCurdy
Associate Curator Ceramics

FIGURE. 87
Alice M. Egan Hagen
(1872 - 1972)
Jug, 1910
Hand painted porcelain, 16.2 x 24.0 x 17.5 cm
Gift of the Estate of Ralph Townsend and family in memory of Ralph and Marion Townsend, Halifax, Nova Scotia, 2001
2001.45

FIGURE. 88
Homer Lord
Canadian (1922 - 1994)
Covered Jardinière, c.1980
Earthenware, 20.5 x 15.0 x 15.0 cm
Purchase, 1994
1994.265

FIGURE. 89
Walter Ostrom
Canadian (b. 1944)
Fish Vase with Greek Pot, 1990
Earthenware, resist and polychrome glaze, 25.0 x 26.5 x 8.5 cm
Purchase, 1994
1994.264

FIGURE. 90
Brother Thomas
Canadian (b. 1929)
Large Globular Vase, 1992
Porcelain with copper red glaze, 33.5 x 31.5 x 31.5 cm
Gift of the Artist and the Pucker Gallery, Boston, Mass.,
in memory of Fritz Webber, 1993
1993.80

FIGURE. 91
Alison Britton
British (b. 1948)
Blue Apron Pot, 1997
Earthenware, 47.0 x 38.0 x 34.5 cm
Purchased with funds provided by Dover Mills Limited and the support of Lauder Brunton, Jean Shaw, Aida Milller Arnold, Mona Campbell, Darrel and Elizabeth Pink and Karen Farquhar, 2000
2000.16

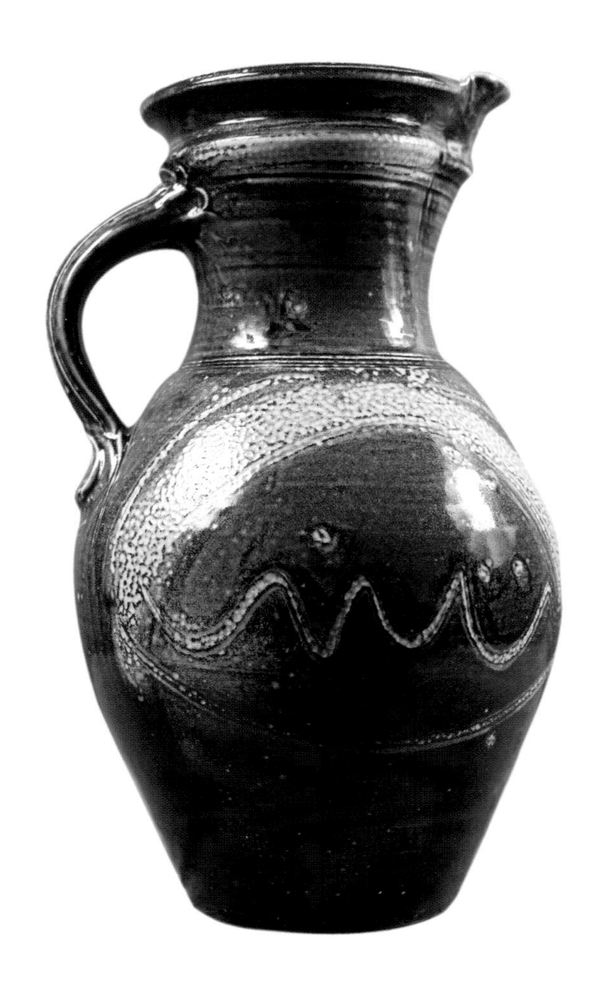

FIGURE. 92
Michael Casson
British (b. 1925)
Jug, 1998
Stoneware, salt-glazed, 47.0 x 30.0 x 28.0 cm
Purchase, 1998
1998.360

FIGURE. 93
Les Manning
Canadian (b. 1944)
Majestic Ridge, 1999
Laminated stoneware and porcelain, 28.5 x 30.5 x 25.5 cm
Purchase, 2000
2000.49

FIGURE. 94
Wayne Higby
American (b. 1943)
Monument Beach, 1999
Earthenware, 20.0 x 21.5 x 8.0 cm
Purchase, 1999
1999.145

FIGURE. 95
Jean-Pierre Larocque
Canadian (b. 1953)
Untitled, 2000
White stoneware fired to Cone 1, 73.5 x 68.0 x 31.0 cm
Purchased with the support of the Canada Council for the Arts Acquisition Assistance Program, the Art Sales and Rental Society and the Friends of the Art Gallery of Nova Scotia, 2000
2000.181

FIGURE. 96
Andrea Gill
American (b. 1948)
Deruta's Geisha Vase, 2001
Earthenware, 78.8 x 40.5 x 28.3 cm
Purchase, 2001
2001.110

HISTORICAL PRINTS AND DRAWINGS

HISTORICAL PRINTS AND DRAWINGS

The great print and drawing collections in Canada were formed long before the Art Gallery of Nova Scotia was established in 1975. The 123 prints and drawings previously acquired by the NSMFA comprised half its entire collection, and that proportion was largely maintained in the AGNS collection until 1995. The donation of 3,000 sheets by John and Norma Oyler between 1995 and 1998 has made prints and drawings the fastest growing section of the Permanent Collection. For the most part, the 6,500 prints and drawings in the collection today can only indicate the work of outstanding artists or important movements and the techniques associated with them, rather than comprehensively represent any one aspect in depth. The major exception lies in the realm of Nova Scotian topographical prints, which formed the core of the Oyler collection and which have enabled a continuing series of exhibitions in the Early Canadian Prints and Drawings Gallery.

During its first ten years, the NSMFA had purchased two watercolours from retiring VSAD principal Georges Chavignaud, and four etchings by artists associated with the etching revival in Canada—Thomas Garland Green, Herbert Raine, Dorothy Stevens, and Nova Scotia's own Lewis Smith—and received one watercolour, a bequest, by a prominent English painter, Thomas Faed. A sporadic pattern of individual purchases or donations, primarily of watercolours or drawings by Nova Scotian artists, continued through the next fifty years. The two exceptional instances were the acquisition of a set of Arthur Lismer's fifteen war lithographs by purchase from the government and donation from the artist in 1919, and the donation of a collection of Lewis Smith's etchings by his widow, following his death in 1926. Smith, a charter member of the NSMFA, had served as principal of the VSAD between 1910 and 1912. *Barges at Hammersmith* (Fig. 114) had been exhibited at the Provincial Exhibition in 1913; Smith revisited this theme in 1917 for another plate, variously titled *Loading the Thames Barge* and *Unloading Barges, Hammersmith.*

In 1967, following the establishment of the Centennial Gallery, the gift of the Centennial Collection of the Nova Scotia Society of Artists, which included five watercolours, reactivated the prints and drawings section. Additional impetus came in 1972 with the gift of forty-four prints by contemporary British artists from Alistair McAlpine (later Lord McAlpine of West Green). The McApline gift also included four serigraph prints by Painters 11 member Jack Bush. In *Low Sun* (Fig. 123), Bush plays with the relationship of colour to its environment, an idea he was exploring in his paintings at that time. Lord McAlpine's generous recognition of the new gallery encouraged the donation of several contemporary and historical prints and drawings over the next few years. This activity culminated, a few months before legislation created the Art Gallery of Nova Scotia in 1975, with LeRoy and Marguerite Zwicker's donation of one etching by Gyrth Russell, a Nova Scotian printmaker active during the early years of the century, and another by Rembrandt. The LeRoy Zwicker bequest included a second Rembrandt etching, *Christ Driving the Money Changers from the Temple* (Fig. 97), in 1987. In 1975, the scope of the print and drawing collection inherited by the AGNS lay primarily in twentieth-century Canadian and international works, backed by a small selection of historical pieces in both areas.

The McAlpine gift, made shortly before the AGNS officially opened its doors, was paralleled soon after by an equally generous donation from Neil Phillips of Hiroshige's *Fifty-three Stations of the Tokaido* (Fig. 106). Over the next few years, collection acquisitions included NSCA graduate Charles Parker's *Shipyard*, which indicated the 1930s etching revival in the province, Dorothy Steven's pastel study for the Art Gallery of Ontario's *Nude and Palm Tree*, lithographs by Picasso and Käthe Kollwitz, and several works by Miller Brittain. A later gift of Brittain's *Torsos* (Fig. 121) by the Teichert estate extended his representation in the collection. The death of former NSCA principal Donald Cameron Mackay (Fig. 116) in 1979 occasioned the collection's acquisition of nineteen of his etchings as a gift from Margot Mackay, and a later gift of nineteen miniature portraits of British, European, and Maritime subjects from his collection.

The print and drawing holdings doubled in the mid-1980s with the gift from Harold Giddens of 144 historical prints and maps, ranging from Currier & Ives' *Nova Scotia Scenery* (Fig. 112), and one of James Pattison Cockburn's Montreal views, to wood engravings from the *Illustrated London News*. A further leap was occasioned by the gift from Nelly Beveridge Gray of 158 rubbings she had made at sites throughout Asia, Africa, and Mesoamerica. Canadian representation in the collection was enhanced by the acquisition of watercolours such as Pegi Nicol MacLeod's *Street Scene* (Fig. 117) and William Brymner's *Fieldhands* from 1905, and of prints such as Christopher Pratt's *Ice* from 1972 and Joyce Wieland's *O Canada* from 1970 (Fig. 122), one of the first prints pulled by the NSCAD Lithography Workshop. Her print, the gift of Dr. George Holbrook, is a series of passionate kisses that affirm a low-key affectionate patriotism. The AGNS does not possess a complete set of the NSCAD lithos, but, as the repository for the Loan-collection of the Nova Scotia College of Art and Design, we are able to include any of them in permanent collection installations. The Giddens gift of historical Canadian prints was soon balanced by the acquisition of the Conrod-Jakabos Collection of 574 European prints, the gift of Hugh and Suzanne Conrod. A newspaper photographer early in his career, Conrod developed an interest in the production of images prior to the advent of modern technology.

The various print media, rather than the artists or their subjects, were the basis for his collection. The range of the Conrod-Jakabos Collection is considerable. It includes the two volumes of etchings produced by Bartolozzi and his followers of drawings in the British Royal Collection, and the bound set of French engravings after Peter Paul Rubens' designs for the Marie de Medici paintings at the Luxembourg Palace. As well, it includes other works engraved by Bartolozzi in his characteristic stipple manner, such as Angelica Kauffmann's *Cornelia, Mother of the Gracchi* (Fig. 99); complete sets of William Hogarth's *The Rake's Progress* and *Marriage à la Mode;* and isolated single sheets, such as *Ophelia* (Fig. 113) by the American Pre-Raphaelite, Anna Lea Merritt.

To commemorate the AGNS move to its present downtown site, Richard and Jocelyn Raymond donated a suite of thirteen watercolour drawings of Halifax and vicinity (Fig. 109), executed in the late 1850s by Gaspard LeMarchant Tupper. The LeMarchant Tupper drawings have since been complemented by a set of twenty-one views of the region taken a decade earlier by Sir Michael Seymour (Fig. 108), while he served as captain of Sir Francis Austen's flagship. The purchase of the Seymour drawings received generous funding in 1998 from the Government of Canada under the terms of the Cultural Property Export and Import Act, and from Templeton Management Inc. The Cultural Property Export Review Board had earlier supported the Gallery's purchase of two important watercolours: Edward Hicks' *The Entrance to Halifax Harbour and the Town of Halifax* (Fig. 101) in 1990, and Westcott Witchurch Lyttleton's *Halifax Harbour Seen from McNab's Island* in 1988. The inclusion of three watercolours of Mik'maq subjects (Fig. 102) among the Christopher Ondaatje gift in 1994, and the simultaneous purchase of Joseph Brown Comingo's 1816 *View of Windsor, taken from Sanford's* (Fig. 105) further consolidated the strength of historical Nova Scotian material in the collection.

In 1992, the Gallery again received generous support from the Cultural Property Export Review Board for the repatriation of Emily Carr's *Deep in the Woods* (Fig. 118), an exuberant study of the British Columbia rain forest, executed in her idiosyncratic oil-and-gasoline-on-manilla-paper method. Three watercolours by longtime gallery supporter Marguerite Zwicker came into the collection on the artist's death in 1994. *Patricia* (Fig. 119), the only portrait among these, conveys a sense of the confidence and strength achieved by the New Woman during World War II. The gift from Jack and Joan Craig of a pastel drawing by Newfoundland-born Maurice Cullen (Fig. 115) that year increased our representation of important Canadian artists. Chris Huntington and Charlotte McGill also favoured the AGNS with a collection of Canadian art in 1998, including Jack Humphrey's *Abstract* (Fig. 120), a study of movement through colour alone. During the 1990s, the twentieth-century holdings were further strengthened by a gift from the Nova Scotia Printmakers Association of twenty-two recent prints in various media pulled by their members. As well, the AGNS became the repository in this decade of portfolios of prints and preliminary drawings that trace the printmaking practices of Henry Orenstein and Roger Savage, two outstanding artists resident in the province.

The print and drawing department had always maintained a tenuous balance among historical Canadian, twentieth-century Canadian, and historical European art over the century (with a smaller Oriental section that had grown up around the Hiroshige woodcuts), but the weight of the collection became firmly fixed in its historical Canadian component with the donation, beginning in 1995, of over 3,000 prints and drawings by John and Norma Oyler. The Oyler's collection had assembled examples of topographical printmaking by Nova Scotians, and of Nova Scotia, from the earliest views and maps produced by Champlain at the beginning of the seventeenth century, to wood engravings from the *Canadian Illustrated News* and other illustrated magazines at the end of the nineteenth (Fig. 110). Their gift has provided the AGNS with the firm base on which to build a comprehensive collection for the study of Nova Scotian prints.

Included in the gift are George Isham Parkyns' set of aquatints depicting Halifax in 1800 (Fig. 103); the original drawing for a print in the *Naval Chronicle* of George's Island (Fig. 104), suites of engravings and lithographs produced by William Eagar in the late 1830s, and those by his contemporary, Robert Petley (Fig. 107); Maria Morris Miller's lithographs depicting the wild flowers of Nova Scotia (Fig. 111); a still-growing collection of Nova Scotian views prepared by Joseph Frederick Wallet DesBarres for the *Atlantic Neptune* (Fig. 100); and 272 maps ranging from the famous *Porcupine Map* (Fig. 98) of early Halifax to bird's-eye views of Nova Scotian towns and cities in the late nineteenth century. With continuing generosity, John Oyler has supported the Gallery's purchase of such works as John Stevenet Clow's 1851 drawing of the *Parade Ground*, and his 1852 lithograph of the Church Built In A Day, as they have become available.

The most recent purchase for the Prints and Drawings section, a panoramic watercolour in sepia of the *Halifax Shipyard* painted in 1920 by the American artist Richard W. Rummell, confirms the fundamental priority of the collection: representing the cultural heritage of this region to the people of Nova Scotia.

Mora Dianne O'Neill
Associate Curator Historical Prints and Drawings

FIGURE. 97
Rembrandt Harmensz Van Rijn
Dutch (1606 - 1669)
Christ Driving the Money Changers from the Temple, 1635
Etching, 13.6 x 16.9 cm
Gift of the Estate of LeRoy J. Zwicker, Halifax, Nova Scotia, 1987
1987.99

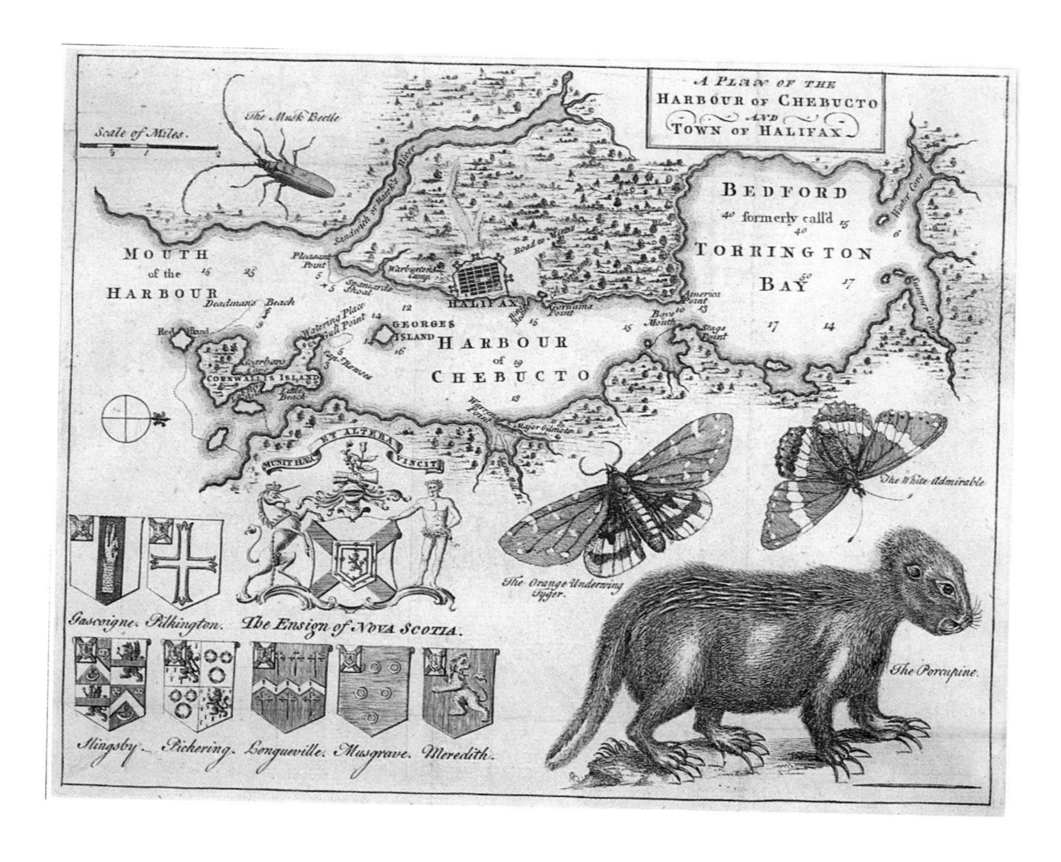

FIGURE. 98
Moses Harris
British (1731 - 1785)
A Plan of the Harbour of Chebucto and Town of Halifax (*The Porcupine Map*), 1750
Hand-coloured engraving, 24.0 x 28.9 cm
Gift of John and Norma Oyler, Halifax, Nova Scotia, 1998
1998.592

FIGURE. 99
Francesco Bartolozzi
Italian/British (1725 - 1815)
after Angelica Kauffmann
Swiss/British (1741 - 1807)
Cornelia, Mother of the Gracchi, c.1775
Coloured stipple engraving, 35.8 x 43.8 cm
Gift of Hugh and Suzanne Conrod, Dartmouth, Nova Scotia,
in memory of Julian Jakabos, 1989
(Conrod-Jakabos Collection)
1989.181

FIGURE. 100
Joseph Frederick Wallet DesBarres
Canadian (1722 - 1824)
A View of the Town and Harbour of Halifax from Dartmouth Shore, 1781
Aquatint in sepia, 37.4 x 56.2 cm
Gift of John and Norma Oyler, Halifax, Nova Scotia, 2001
2001.40

FIGURE. 101
Lieutenant-Colonel Edward Hicks
American (c.1740 - after 1792)
Entrance to Halifax Harbour and the Town of Halifax, Nova Scotia, c.1780
Pencil, ink, and watercolour on paper, 16.5 x 34.5 cm
Purchased with funds provided by the Government of Canada
under the terms of the Cultural Property Export and Import Act, Ottawa, 1990
1990.62

FIGURE. 102
Unknown, possibly John Cunningham
Canadian (c.1723 - 1791)
Mi'kmaq Chief and European Visitor (*Micmac Indians Conversing with a European*), c. 1790
Watercolour on paper, 23.0 x 34.5 cm
Gift of Christopher Ondaatje, Toronto, Ontario, 1994
1994.229

FIGURE. 103
George Isham Parkyns
British (1750 - 1820)
View of Halifax from George's Island, 1801
Hand-coloured aquatint, 34.0 x 53.5 cm
Gift of John and Norma Oyler, Halifax, Nova Scotia, 1998
1998.412

FIGURE. 104
JE, possibly Robert James Elliott
British (1790 - 1849)
St George's Island, Halifax Harbour, c.1806
Ink wash on paper, 14.5 x 27.0 cm
Gift of John and Norma Oyler, Halifax, Nova Scotia, 1995
1995.205

FIGURE. 105
Joseph Brown Comingo
Canadian (1784 - 1821)
View of Windsor, taken from Sandford's, 1816
Watercolour on paper, 21.0 x 37.6 cm
Purchased, 1994
1994.200

FIGURE. 106
Utagawa Hiroshige
Japanese (1797 - 1858)
Nihonbashi: Morning Scene from *Fifty-three Stations of the Tokaido*, c.1834
Colour woodblock, 23.8 x 36.1 cm
Gift of Neil Phillips, QC, Montréal, Quebéc, 1976
1976.36

FIGURE. 107
Robert Petley
British (1812 - 1869)
View on the Banks of the Shubenacadie, 1836
Hand-coloured lithograph on chine collé, 16.8 x 24.6 cm
Gift of John and Norma Oyler, Halifax, Nova Scotia, 1995
1995.80.4

FIGURE. 108
Captain Michael Seymour
British (1802 - 1887)
Shultz Inn on the Grand Lake, Halifax, 1846
Watercolour on paper, 18.0 x 25.6 cm
Purchased with funds provided by the Government of Canada
under the terms of the Cultural Property Export and Import Act, Ottawa,
and Templeton Management Inc., Toronto, Ontario, 1998
1998.308

FIGURE. 109
Gaspard LeMarchant Tupper
British (1826 - 1906)
St. Paul's Church and Dalhousie College from the South-East, c.1855
Watercolour on paper, 16.1 x 34.5 cm
Gift of Richard and Jocelyn Raymond, Halifax, Nova Scotia, 1987
1987.50

FIGURE. 110
James Fox Bland
British (1827 - 1893)
"Coasting" at Halifax, Nova Scotia, 1859
Hand-coloured wood engraving, 25.9 x 37.5 cm
Gift of John and Norma Oyler, Halifax, Nova Scotia, 1998
1998.433

FIGURE. 111
Maria Morris Miller
Canadian (1813 - 1875)
White Water Lily, 1867
Hand-coloured lithograph, 30.8 x 25.5 cm
Gift of John and Norma Oyler, Halifax, Nova Scotia, 1995
1995.90

FIGURE. 112
unknown artist for Currier & Ives
American (19th century)
Nova Scotia Scenery, 1868
Hand-coloured lithograph, 19.3 x 43.5 cm
Gift of Harold Giddens, Halifax, Nova Scotia, 1984
1984.236

FIGURE. 113
Anna Lea Merritt
American (1844 - 1930)
Ophelia, 1880
Etching, 33.3 x 23.8 cm
Gift of Hugh and Suzanne Conrod, Dartmouth, Nova Scotia,
in memory of Julian Jakabos, 1989
(Conrod-Jakabos Collection)
1989.166

FIGURE. 114
Lewis Edward Smith
Canadian (1871 - 1926)
Barges at Hammersmith, 1913
Etching 24/50, 21.8 x 16.3 cm
Purchased 1917
1931.1

FIGURE. 115
Maurice Galbraith Cullen
Canadian (1866 - 1934)
Early Spring, St. Margaret's, 1925
Pastel on paper, 61.0 x 82.6 cm
Gift of Jack and Joan Craig, Halifax, Nova Scotia, 1997
1997.169

FIGURE. 116
Donald Cameron Mackay
Canadian (1906 - 1979)
Building a Bluenose (*Shipyard, Lunenburg*), c.1930
Etching, 9.3 x 15.7 cm
Gift of Margot Mackay, Toronto, Ontario, 1980
1980.88

FIGURE. 117
Pegi Nicol MacLeod
Canadian (1904 - 1949)
Street Scene, c.1935
Watercolour on paper, 50.8 x 34.4 cm
Gift of Marguerite and LeRoy Zwicker, Halifax, Nova Scotia, 1984
1984.3

FIGURE. 118
Emily Carr
Canadian (1871 - 1945)
Deep in the Woods, c.1936
Oil on manilla paper, 89.0 x 31.0 cm
Purchased with funds provided by the Government of Canada under the terms of the Cultural Property Export and Import Act, Ottawa, and the AGNS Volunteer Committee, 1992
1992.10

FIGURE. 119
Marguerite Porter Zwicker
Canadian (1904 - 1993)
Patricia, 1941
Watercolour on paper, 35.0 x 35.0 cm
Gift of the Estate of Marguerite Zwicker, Halifax, Nova Scotia, 1994
1994.43

FIGURE. 120
Jack Weldon Humphrey
Canadian (1901 - 1967)
Abstract, c.1950
Ink and watercolour on paper, 56.4 x 73.2 cm
Gift of Chris Huntington and Charlotte McGill, Mahone Bay, Nova Scotia, 1998
1998.354

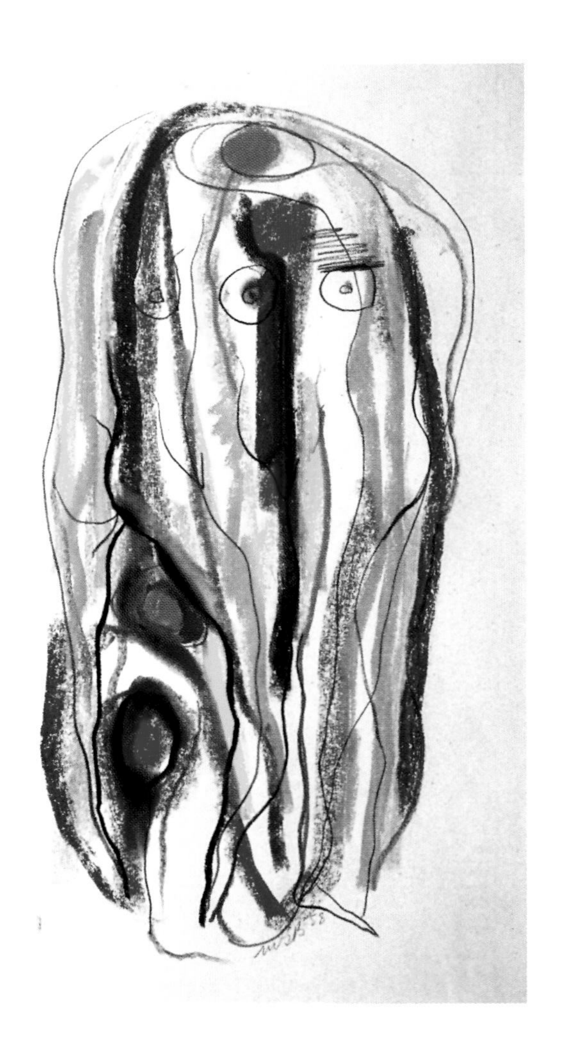

FIGURE. 121
Miller Gore Brittain
Canadian (1912 - 1968)
Torsos, 1958
Pastel and pencil on paper, 45.5 x 30.5 cm
Given in memory of Irma MacQuarrie Teichert, Halifax,
by her daughters, Barbara, Melita, and Gillian Teichert, 1991
1991.46

FIGURE. 122
Joyce Wieland
Canadian (1931 - 1998)
O Canada, 1970
Lithograph 45/60, 57.4 x 76.6 cm
Gift of Dr. George W. Holbrook, Tantallon, Nova Scotia, 1985
1985.31

FIGURE. 123
Jack Bush
Canadian (1909 - 1977)
Low Sun, 1971
Serigraph 4/100, 85.2 x 64.1 cm
Gift of Alistair McAlpine, London, England, 1972
1972.2

INTERNATIONAL PAINTING AND SCULPTURE

INTERNATIONAL PAINTING AND SCULPTURE

The basic strength of the International collection reflects the history of the province and rests in European and British art and, to a lesser degree, American. Since the Art Gallery of Nova Scotia's acquisition mandate focuses on Nova Scotian and Canadian art, works by international artists are only acquired as donations, unless they enjoy a direct connection to the history of the province. The AGNS inherited a small collection of international paintings from the Nova Scotia Museum of Fine Arts which has increased seven-fold over the preceding quarter-century. Most were acquired through the kindness of generous benefactors and represent their personal tastes and interests. Special federal and provincial grants and other fund-raising efforts have allowed the Gallery to purchase significant works with close historical ties to Nova Scotia, and to Halifax in particular. Works from this collection are featured in the City of Halifax Gallery, the Alice Hoskins Gallery of International Art, and the Laufer Family Gallery.

Classical Roman art is a rarity in Canadian collections. Our collection at the AGNS is graced by a *Head of the Emperor Augustus* (Fig. 124), by an unknown artist from the first century C.E., which depicts Augustus as a man of power and intellect, serenity and magnetism. Despite damage to the nose, it conveys tranquillity and classical symmetry. Probably a remnant from a version of the *Augustus of Prima Porta* now in the Vatican, it was excavated in 1884 and purchased by Dr. Immanuel Friedlander from a gallery in Rome in 1903; through inheritance, the *Head* came to Canada in 1934 and was given to us by the Laufer family in 1992.

One of the finest pieces of mediaeval sculpture in Canada is our fifteenth-century fragment of *The Crucifixion* (Fig. 125), carved by an unknown Netherlandish artist. Brought to Nova Scotia by Bishop William Walsh in the 1840s, the *Crucifixion* and two smaller reliefs depicting scenes from the *Passion of Christ* were installed in the Chapel Built in a Day in 1843. Following fifteen years (9,000 hours) of extensive restoration by the Canadian Conservation Institute in Ottawa, these works were gifted to the AGNS by the Archdiocese of Halifax. Offering a compelling and intimate image of human dignity and suffering, the *Crucifixion* fragment focuses on the Virgin Mary, dramatically fainting at the sight of her son's suffering. Behind her, John the Evangelist reaches for a swathe of linen and Mary Magdalene, turning away from the viewer, extends her arms in grief toward the dead Christ who once hung above the walls and towers of the city of Jerusalem. The fashionable turban-style headdresses and attire reflect Dutch or Flemish costume from the period between 1470 and 1490. The small rounded faces, diminutive mouths, almond-shaped eyes, and curly hair of the figures are characteristic of sculpture from Malines (Mechelen, in Flemish), stylistically described as "les poupées de Malines." Their idealized beauty and graceful elegance is enhanced by their elongated proportions.

A similar elongation of the human figure characterizes the sixteenth-century painting, *Madonna and Child with St John the Baptist* (Fig. 126), attributed to the Italian artist Giulio Romano. A painter and architect in the Mannerist style, Giulio was Raphael's favoured protégé, who assisted his master on the murals in the Vatican. Following Raphael's death, he moved to Mantua. Particularly charming in this *Madonna* is the artist's interpretation of the mother, who tries to restrain her son by grasping his drapery. From his seat on a sarcophagus, the Christ Child reaches towards the kneeling St. John, who gazes toward him in adoration. The three figures are set in front of a portal, suggesting the entrance to a tomb. The image thus foreshadows the Child's predestined fate, his ministry, and his death.

The Neapolitan school is represented in the AGNS collection by two romantic landscapes by Salvator Rosa, entitled *Rocky Landscape With Figures* (Fig. 127) and *Landscape With Two Soldiers and Ruins* (Fig. 128). Both are typical of Rosa's depictions of banditti figures in wild-forested and mountainous settings. Part of a collection purchased and assembled by Joseph Allen Smith of South Carolina in 1797, and destined as a gift to the new Pennsylvania Academy of the Fine Arts, the paintings were shipped off to the United States during the War of 1812 in a French vessel which was captured by the British navy and brought to Halifax as a prize of war. The Academy entered a petition for the release of the artworks before Sir Alexander Croke, Vice-Admiralty Court Judge in Halifax. Croke's decision on April 21, 1813, citing the law of nations as practiced by civilized countries, declared works of art to be exempt from the spoils of war. A reference to Croke's unprecedented decision appeared in the preamble of the *Hague Convention for the Protection of Cultural Property in the Event of Armed Conflict* in 1954. In recognition of his enlightened decision in 1813, the Academy, through the American Consul General, presented the two Salvator Rosa paintings to the NSMFA in 1952, as a token of peace and friendship between our two nations.

Although Nova Scotia shares the common artistic inheritance from Europe of all Western countries, its historical and cultural ties to Great Britain are naturally more pronounced, and works by British artists form the major part of our international holdings. Among the earliest known paintings of a Canadian city, *Governor's House and St. Mather's Meeting House on Hollis Street also Looking up George Street* (Fig. 129) was painted by Dominic Serres, based on Richard Short's 1759 sketches of the town and harbour of Halifax. Depicted are the Governor's House in the centre (site of Province House today), the dissident Protestant meeting house on the left, and St. Paul's Anglican Church with part of the Parade

Grounds and Citadel Hill in the background. Though born in France, Serres spent most of his working life as a painter in England. A founding member of the Royal Academy, and Marine Painter to King George III, he painted seascapes and naval actions in minute detail. His four Halifax views are imbued with an air of romance and the subtle tonalities produced by sea-governed atmospherics.

Sir Joshua Reynolds, who painted *George Montagu Dunk, Second Earl of Halifax,* (Fig. 130), is considered the greatest and most influential of all British portrait artists. Known for endowing his sitters in grand style with dignity and elegance, Reynolds became the first president of the Royal Academy of the Arts in 1768. In an effort to imitate techniques of the old masters, Reynolds experimented with painting materials. The fading, cracking, and bluish-grey pallor that so often followed is evident in our *Halifax* portrait. George Montagu Dunk, the Second Earl of Halifax, was known as the "Father of the Colonies" for his role in expanding the British presence in North America. Governor Edward Cornwallis named the town of Halifax after him in 1749. Painted in 1764, the three-quarter portrait shows the Earl of Halifax in ceremonial robes, wearing a white wig and collar, a riband, and the Star of the Garter. An impressive portrait of commanding presence, the painting was originally commissioned from Reynolds by Pole Cosby, whose aunt was the Earl's sister.

One of the most accomplished artists ever to work in Halifax, Robert Field was born and educated in England. After working in various American cities along the eastern seaboard as an engraver and miniature portraitist between 1794 and 1808, Field spent eight years in Halifax, where he received numerous commissions from government officials and from the mercantile and naval classes. He returned to England in 1816 and later died in Jamaica. Painted in 1813, his three-quarter portrait of *Lieutenant Provo William Parry Wallis* (Fig. 131) portrays a gallant and distinguished naval officer. The highlights on his forehead and nose, and the unrestrained wavy locks of hair, together with the turbulent clouds in the background, afford the portrait an air of freshness and romance. A more sedate and classical version of the portrait is in the National Gallery of Canada's collection. Provo Wallis was born in Halifax, the son of Provo Featherstone Wallis, whose portrait by Field is one of eight also in the AGNS collection. The younger Wallis was involved in the famous victory over the American frigate, *Chesapeake,* off the coast of Boston in 1813. Wallis took command of the *Shannon* after the wounding of Captain Philip Broke and carried his prize triumphantly back to Halifax. He was knighted in 1869 and became Admiral of the Fleet in 1877, the first Canadian-born naval officer to hold that position.

Shipping at Low Tide, Halifax (Fig. 132), attributed to the British artist John Poad Drake, portrays a romantic view of Halifax Harbour at sunset, with the shores of Halifax and Dartmouth in the background. In the foreground, Mi'kmaq vendors are bartering on the shores of George's Island, while a Mi'kmaq canoe, a full-rigged ship, and a topsail schooner may be seen on the harbour. John Poad Drake, a direct descendant of Sir Francis Drake, was born in Devonshire, England. He came as an itinerant artist to Halifax, Charlottetown, Montreal, New York, and other American cities, before returning to England in 1828 to work as a naval draughtsman, architect, and inventor.

Geographical proximity links Nova Scotia culturally and historically to the United States. One of the outstanding American paintings in the collection is *Ship Nathaniel Hooper* (Fig. 133) by the American marine artist, Fitz Hugh Lane. Considered one of the foremost American Luminist painters, Lane created a poetic interpretation of the sea through his rendering of atmosphere and light, a skill he may have developed as a lithographer in Pendleton's Boston shop. Commissioned in 1861 by part-owner Benjamin Porter at the time of its launching, *Ship Nathaniel Hooper* is executed with Lane's customary detail and precision. The Nathaniel Hooper is shown in profile with sails partially unfurled. The artist establishes a tranquil and contemplative mood with a pale sky, hazy yet radiant, and with gentle ripples along the shoreline of the mirror-like waters.

A very different tranquillity invests *Study for Homage to the Square, "Teen-Age"* (Fig. 134) by the German-born Josef Albers. He immigrated to the United States after the Nazi closure of the Bauhaus school at Weimar, and began experimenting with the subtle effects and perceptual properties of pure colour, with the interaction of light and colour within geometric frames. During the 1950s and '60s, he developed his *Homage to the Square* series, in which he explored the relationship of colour squares confined within other squares. *Study for Homage to the Square, "Teen-Age"* effectively demonstrates this interaction of colour and straight lines. Albers has influenced generations of artists worldwide, particularly those working in the movements of Constructivism, Minimalism, and Op Art.

The Art Gallery of Nova Scotia is pleased to supplement and enrich its Canadian holdings by providing visitors and members with exposure to works from outside Canada. The journey of art through time and place, or provenance, has its own special significance, and can be as intriguing as the actual artwork and artist. We are fortunate to be custodian of such a diverse and significant collection of international art.

Judy Dietz
Manager of Collections/Registrar

FIGURE. 124
Unknown
Roman
Head of the Emperor Augustus, 1st century C.E.
Marble, 29.0 x 22.5 x 24.0 cm
Gift of Dr. and Mrs. S.T. Laufer, Halifax, Nova Scotia, 1992
1992.37

FIGURE. 125
Unknown (Malines Region, Belgium)
Flemish
The Crucifixion, c.1470 - 1490 (detail)
Polychrome wood, 101.0 x 41.0 x 22.0 cm
Gift of the Archdiocese of Halifax, from the Church of Seven Dolores of the Blessed Virgin Mary, Chapel Built in a Day, Halifax, Nova Scotia, 1996
1996.147

FIGURE. 126
Attributed to Giulio Romano
Italian (c.1499 - 1546)
Madonna and Child with St. John the Baptist, 16th century
Oil on panel, 68.0 x 53.5 cm.
Gift of Dr. and Mrs. S.T. Laufer, Halifax, Nova Scotia, 1997
1998.389

FIGURE. 127
Salvator Rosa
Italian (1615 - 1673)
Rocky Landscape with Figures, c.1650
Oil on canvas, 51.3 x 66.4 cm
Gift of the United States of America in recognition of the historic 1813 decision by the Honourable Sir Alexander Croke, Justice of the Court of Vice-Admiralty, Halifax, respecting prizes of war. Presented by the United States Consul-General at Halifax, 1952
1952.1

FIGURE. 128
Salvator Rosa
Italian (1615 - 1673)
Landscape with Two Soldiers and Ruins, c.1650
Oil on canvas, 50.4 x 66.4 cm

Gift of the United States of America in recognition of the historic 1813 decision by the Honourable Sir Alexander Croke, Justice of the Court of Vice-Admiralty, Halifax, respecting prizes of war. Presented by the United States Consul-General at Halifax, 1952
1952.2

FIGURE. 129
Dominic Serres
British (1719 - 1793)
Governor's House and St. Mather's Meeting House on Hollis Street, also looking up George Street, c.1762
Oil on canvas, 38.1 x 55.9 cm
Purchased with funds provided by the Gallery's Art Trust Fund (Mrs. Stewart L. Gibson Bequest), The Cultural Foundation of Nova Scotia, and private and corporate donations, 1982
1982.41

FIGURE. 130
Sir Joshua Reynolds, P.R.A.
British (1723 - 1792)
Portrait of George Montagu Dunk, 2nd Earl of Halifax, K.G., 1764
Oil on canvas, 76.0 x 63.2 cm
Purchased with funds provided by the Government of Canada under the terms of the Cultural Property Export and Import Act, Ottawa, the Nova Scotia Department of Culture, Recreation and Fitness and LeRoy J. Zwicker, Halifax, Nova Scotia, 1984
1984.33

FIGURE. 131
Robert Field
British (c.1769 - 1819)
Lieutenant Provo William Parry Wallis (1791-1892), 1813
Oil on canvas, 76.2 x 63.5 cm
Purchase, 1979
1979.18

FIGURE. 132
Attributed to John Poad Drake
British (1794 - 1883)
Shipping at Low Tide, c.1820
Oil on canvas, 68.6 x 97.8 cm
Purchase, 1984. Dedicated to the memory of Evan Petley-Jones, 1945 - 1996
1994.258

FIGURE. 133
Fitz Hugh Lane
American (1804 - 1865)
Ship Nathaniel Hooper, 1861
Oil on canvas, 51.0 x 76.5 cm
Gift of Lauder Brunton, in memory of his wife Marjorie,
Guysborough, Nova Scotia, 1999
1999.246

FIGURE. 134
Josef Albers
American (1888 - 1976)
Study for Homage to the Square, "Teen Age", 1961
Oil on masonite, 60.5 x 60.5 cm
Gift of Marjorie and Lauder Brunton, Guysborough, Nova Scotia, 1993
1993.104

LIST OF ARTISTS

Albers, Josef 188
Angeconeb, Allen 98
Ashevak, Kenojuak 94
Askevold, David 86
Bartolozzi, Francesco 148
Belanger, Lance 100
Bland, James Fox 159
Bond, Marion 47
Borduas, Paul-Émile 49
Boucher, Wayne 81
Boutilier, Ralph 118
Brittain, Miller Gore 170
Britton, Alison 135
Brooks, David J. 99
Bush, Jack 172
Cameron, Eric 65
Cann, Elizabeth Lovitt 43
Carr, Emily 167
Casson, Michael 136
Collins, Gerard 78
Colville, Alex 50
Comingo, Joseph Brown 154
Cook, Walter 119
Cropas, Nyna 76
Cullen, Maurice Galbraith 164
Cunningham, John 151
Currier & Ives 161
Day, Mabel Killam 38
DesBarres, J.F.W. 149
Dickie, Evelyn 120
Doucette, Charles 103
Drake, John Poad 186
Edell, Nancy 71
Eisenhauer, Collins 123
Elliott, Robert James 153
Eyre, Ivan 77
Fafard, Joe 72
Ferguson, Gerald 79
Field, Robert 185
Fisk, Rebecca 88
Forrest, Greg 85
Forrestall, Tom 75
Fraser, Carol Hoorn 69
Frotten, Peter 114
Gallant, Yvon 63
Gill, Andrea 140
Gray, Jack 48
Greer, John 73
Hagen, Alice M. Egan 131
Hammond, Charlotte Wilson 66
Harris, Moses 147
Harvey, George 27
Hertle, James 111
Hicks, Lieutenant-Colonel Edward 150
Higby, Wayne 138
Hiroshige, Utagawa 155
Howard, Sidney 124
Humphrey, Jack Weldon 169
Ipeelee, Osuitok 97
Jackson, A.Y. 42
Johnson, Margaret 96
Jones (Bannerman), Frances 28
Kennedy, Garry Neill 61
Kauffmann, Angelica 148
Lane, Fitz Hugh 187
Larocque, Jean-Pierre 139
Law, C. Anthony 52
Lawson, Ernest 32
Lemieux, Jean Paul 62
Lewis, Maud 116
Lismer, Arthur 33
Livingston, Alex 70
Lohnes, Albert 117
Lord, Homer 132
McCulloch, J. Frederic 39
Macdonald, Charles 112
MacDonald, J.E.H. 34
Mackay, Donald Cameron 165
MacLeod, Pegi Nicol 166
McNicoll, Helen Galloway 31
MacNutt, Dawn 83
Manning, Les 137
Merritt, Anna Lea 162
Miller, Maria Morris 160
Milne, David 41
Morrice, James Wilson 30
Morrisseau, Norval 95
Naugler, Leo 126
Nesbitt, John 67
Norris, Joe 121
Nutt, Elizabeth Styring 35
O'Brien, John 25
Orenstein, Henry 44
Ostrom, Walter 133
Parkyns, George Isham 152
Petley, Robert 156
Poitras, Jane Ash 102
Pratt, Christopher 74
Pratt, Mary 82
Raphael, William 26
Reid, Lorne 125
Rembrandt Harmensz Van Rijn 146
Reynolds, Sir Joshua 184
Riopelle, Jean-Paul 60
Roberts, William Goodridge 51
Romano, Giulio 180
Rosa, Salvator 181, 182
Rosenberg, Henry Mortikar 29
Royle, Stanley 40
Rutherford, Erica 59
Savage, Anne 45
Serres, Dominic 183
Seymour, Captain Michael 157
Shuebrook, Ron 64
Simon, Roger 101
Sleep, Joseph 122
Smith, Edith Agnes 37
Smith, Lewis Edward 163
Syliboy, Alan 104
Tap, Monica 87
Thomas, Brother 134
Tozer (Leefe), Marjorie Hughson 36
Tupper, Gaspard LeMarchant 158
Unknown Nova Scotian artist 113
Unknown Nova Scotian artist 115
Unknown Flemish artist 179
Unknown Roman artist 178
Valentine, William 24
Wainwright, Ruth Salter 68
Wieland, Joyce 171
Wilson, Gary 80
Wolstenholme, Colleen 84
Zwicker, LeRoy Judson 46
Zwicker, Marguerite Porter 168

NOTES ON CONTRIBUTORS

Ray Cronin

Ray Cronin is a graduate of the Nova Scotia College of Art and Design (BFA) and the University of Windsor (MFA). He is the author of several catalogue essays, as well as articles for Canadian and American art magazines. As Curator of Contemporary Art at the Art Gallery of Nova Scotia, Cronin is responsible for organizing all temporary exhibitions, as well as for developing exhibitions for the Gallery. His projects at the AGNS include *Domesticate: David Diviney, Erik Edson, Alexander Graham, Shelly Rahme and Lyla Rye*; *Greg Forrest: Heavy Metal* (with Dale Sheppard, AGNS Educator); *Ruth Wainwright: Selections from a Gift*; and *Cal Lane: Fabricate.*

Judy Dietz

Judy Dietz is Manager of Collections/Registrar at the Art Gallery of Nova Scotia, and is responsible for the Gallery's extensive permanent, study, and loan collections. She has been associated with the AGNS and its predecessor, the Nova Scotia Museum of Fine Arts, since 1973, and has witnessed the growth of the collection from 200 to its current holdings of over 9,000 works of art. She has been the curator for the exhibitions: *An Expression of Faith: Sacred Art of Centuries Past*, and *Carol Hoorn Fraser: Unfinished Business*, and has produced numerous exhibitions from the AGNS European and historical art collections. Dietz is a Master's candidate at Saint Mary's University.

Jim Logan

Following a two year Curatorial Residency at the Art Gallery of Nova Scotia, Jim Logan became Associate Curator First Nations Art, a position he held until his departure in 2001. During his residency, he was curator of three exhibitions: *Mirrored*, *Re-claiming History*, and *Homeboys: Alex Janvier and Alan Syliboy*. As Associate Curator, his exhibition, *Journey*, opened the new First Nations Gallery at the AGNS. He is currently working as the Aboriginal Program Officer in Visual Arts at the Canada Council for the Arts in Ottawa.

Alexandra McCurdy
As Associate Curator Ceramics since 1996, Alexandra McCurdy prepares an annual exhibition for installation in the Lloyd and Jean Shaw Gallery of Ceramics at the Art Gallery of Nova Scotia. These have included *Painterly Ceramics, Earthenware: A Nova Scotia Tradition, Porcelain: A Measure of Mystery,* and *Collectors' Collections* among others. She also chairs the sub-committee for ceramics at the AGNS, which views and makes decisions about future purchases and donations for the Permanent Collection. McCurdy is a practicing ceramist with a national and international exhibition record, and is currently a doctoral candidate at Concordia University in Montreal.

Mora Dianne O'Neill
As Associate Curator Historical Prints and Drawings since 1997, Mora Dianne O'Neill prepares two exhibitions annually for installation in the John and Norma Oyler Gallery of Early Canadian Prints and Drawings at the Art Gallery of Nova Scotia. She served as guest curator of *At the Great Harbour: 250 Years on the Halifax Waterfront,* installed at the AGNS in 1999, and of *Choosing Their Own Path: Canadian Women Impressionists* in 2001. Dr. O'Neill is writing biographical entries on Nova Scotian artists for the new edition of the *Allgemeines Künstlerlexikon* (formerly known as *Thieme-Becker*), and is a contributing writer to *Halifax Street Names: An Illustrated Guide*, 2002.

Bernard Riordon
Bernard Riordon, O.C. is a graduate of Saint Thomas University in Fredericton, and pursued graduate studies at Saint Mary's University in Halifax from 1971 to 1973, that year becoming Curator of the Centennial Art Gallery, Nova Scotia Museum of Fine Arts, with 200 works of art in its collection. In 1975, he became the founding Director of the Art Gallery of Nova Scotia, and has overseen the growth of its Permanent Collection to over 9,000 works. Having provided leadership for the establishment of the AGNS in 1975, for the creation of its first permanent home in downtown Halifax in 1988, and for the Phase II Expansion in 1998, he also initiated the establishment of a satellite gallery, the Western Branch of the Art Gallery of Nova Scotia, in Yarmouth. Exhibitions and catalogues for which he is responsible include: *Nova Scotia Folk Art: Canada's Cultural Heritage, C. Anthony Law: A Retrospective,* and most recently, *Joe Norris: Painted Visions of Nova Scotia.* He has written for magazines and journals, and lectured on art and on cultural administration in Canada and in Europe. Bernard Riordon retired from the AGNS in 2002.